Donja

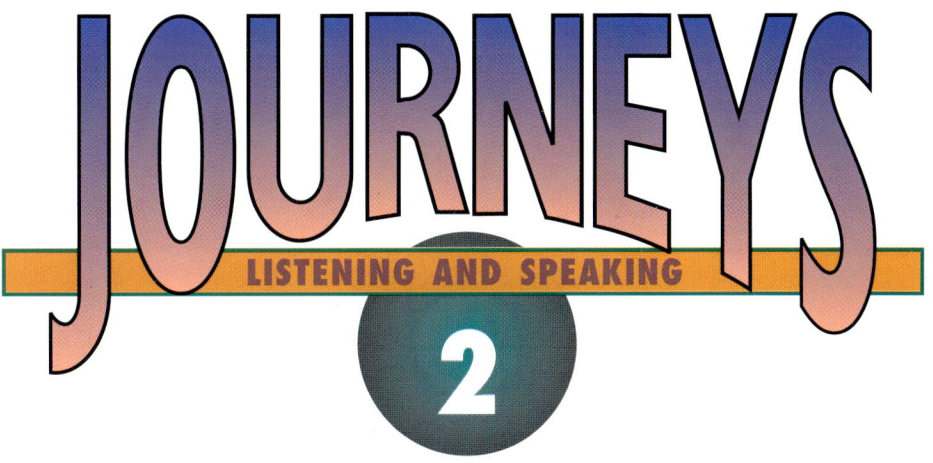

JOURNEYS
LISTENING AND SPEAKING
2

virtual · parkland · edu / eslzine

STACY A. HAGEN

STEVEN BROWN SERIES EDITOR

Prentice Hall ELT

Editorial Director: Marion Cooper
Publisher: Karen Jamieson
Production Manager: Oliver Lam
Design/Illustrations: Lee Meng Hui / Betty Bravo
Cover Photograph: Nick Lutz

First published 2000 by
Prentice Hall ELT
317 Alexandra Road
#04-01 IKEA Building
Singapore 159965

Printed in Singapore

ISBN 0-13-227182-6 (Journeys Listening/Speaking 2)

5 4 3 2 1
04 03 02 01 00

Contents

From the Series Editor

Journeys is a twelve-book, three-level, skills-based series for EFL/ESL learners. The books can be used from beginning level through intermediate level. They parallel the first three levels of basal series, and can be used as supplements to series or as stand-alone skills texts. A unique feature of *Journeys* is that the books can be used to construct a curriculum in those cases where student skills are at different levels. That is, in those classes where reading ability is at a higher level than speaking ability, the teacher is free to choose texts at appropriate levels. Each book can be used separately.

Journeys can be used with high-school-aged students and up.

Journeys takes three notions very seriously:

1. Beginning level students have brains and hearts. They live in an interesting world that they are interested in.

2. Learning needs to be recycled. Rather than work on the same skill or topic across all four books during the same week, topics and language are recycled across the books to keep what students have learned active. Teachers who want to can teach the books out of order because the syllabus of each book progresses slowly.

3. It is possible for beginning level students to work with sophisticated content, yet complete simple tasks. In general, students can understand a much higher level of language than they can produce. By grading tasks, that is, keeping them simple at a beginning level, the linguistic demands made of the students are kept relatively low, but the content of the exercises remains interesting to adult learners.

Steven Brown

Youngstown State University

Acknowledgements

This book is dedicated, with love, to Andy Paterson for the journeys we've had and those yet to come.

The making of this book was indeed a collaborative effort. I would like to express my gratitude to the following people:

- Nancy Baxer, whose vision for this series kept me inspired through the many twists and turns of this rewarding journey;

- Steve Brown, whose extraordinary patience and calm served as a guide from start to finish;

- Guy de Villiers, whose creative energies mark every page;

- Irene Yeow and all the staff at Prentice Hall Asia, whose talent and expertise is reflected throughout.

Stacy Hagen

Photo Credits

UNIT 1 Could You Please Repeat That?

Hwk

Listen and repeat.

What's your name?   Gina Taylor.
How do you spell that?   G-I-N-A T-A-Y-L-O-R.
What's your ID number?   212-4804.
Middle initial?   J.
Birthdate?   8/23/72.
Could you repeat that, please?   Sure. It's 8/23/72.

CONVERSATIONS

Listen and practice.

A. Secretary: Hi, there. Have a seat. What's your name?
    Gladys: Gladys. Gladys Soto.
    Secretary: How do you spell that?
    Gladys: G-L-A-D-Y-S S-O-T-O.
    Secretary: And what's your ID number?
    Gladys: It's 76-432-55.
    Secretary: I'm sorry. Could you please
                repeat that?
    Gladys: Sure, it's 76-432-55.
    Secretary: And which class are you
                registering for?
    Gladys: S/L 2. Is it full?
    Secretary: Not yet. You're in luck.

B. Clerk: I just need a little information. Name?
    Jack: Martin.
    Clerk: Is that your first or last name?
    Jack: Sorry, it's my last. My first name is Jack.
    Clerk: Middle initial?
    Jack: R.
    Clerk: Birthdate?
    Jack: 4/12/62.
    Clerk: That's the same birthday as my sister!

PRACTICE

**Practice conversations A and B with a classmate. Use information about
yourself.**

LISTEN

A. Listen. Circle the letters you hear.

1. (b)   v
2. i   (e)
3. (g)   j
4. (z)   c
5. (e)   i

6. (f)   v
7. u   (w)
8. l   (r)
9. a   (h)
10. t   (d)

B. Listen. Circle the numbers you hear.

1. 923-1492   (923-4092)
2. 6401   (7401)
3. (767-0011)   676-0101
4. (855-8549)   855-9549
5. 1126   (1036)

LISTEN AND UNDERSTAND

Listen. Write the missing words or numbers.

1.

Jun,
Sarah _Berry_
called.
Her number is
_674-9801_.
Please call her.

2.

To: Mr./Mrs./~~Miss~~ _Janus_
Date: _October 3_

WHILE YOU WERE OUT

From: (Mr.)/Mrs./Miss _Mr Williams_
Phone: _565-8100_

Message: _Call as soon as_
possible.

3.

Burlington School

Last name _Choy_

First name _Grace_

Middle name _N M I_

Student ID no. _95-436 2941_

PAIRWORK
STUDENT A

You are registering for a computer course at Future's Computer School. Student B works at the front desk. Answer Student B's questions.

Now ask Student B questions. You work at the front desk of a health clinic. Student B has come for a check up. Ask Student B for information and fill out the form.

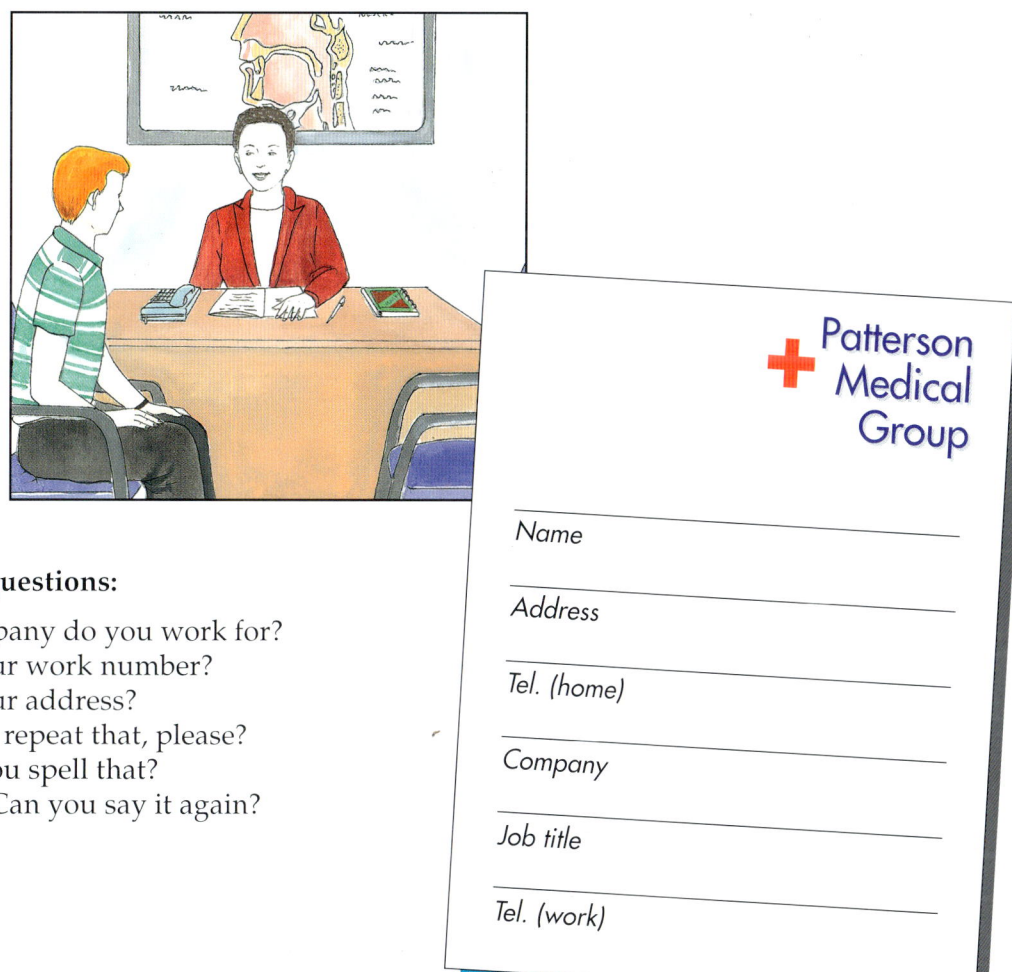

Example questions:

What company do you work for?
What's your work number?
What's your address?
Could you repeat that, please?
How do you spell that?
I'm sorry. Can you say it again?

Patterson
Medical
Group

Name

Address

Tel. (home)

Company

Job title

Tel. (work)

PAIRWORK
STUDENT B

You work at the front desk of Future's Computer School. Student A wants to register for a course. Ask Student A for information and fill out the form.

Example questions:

What company do you work for?
What's your work number?
What's your address?
Could you repeat that, please?
How do you spell that?
I'm sorry. Can you say it again?

FUTURE'S COMPUTER SCHOOL

Name
_____

Company
_____

Job title
_____

Tel. (work)
_____

Address
_____

Tel. (home)
_____

Now you are at a health clinic for a check up. Student A works at the front desk. Answer Student A's questions.

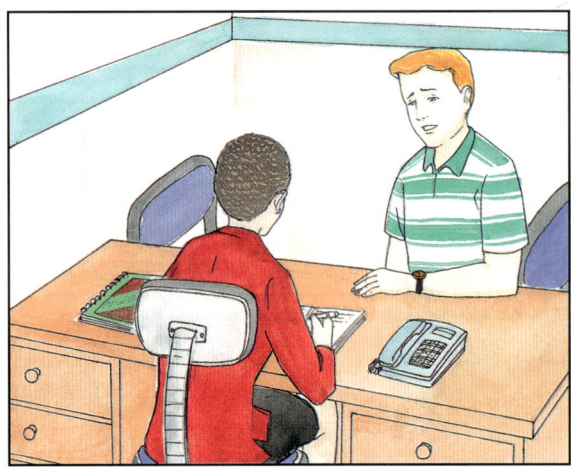

PRONUNCIATION

A. When you spell your name to someone, you need to put the letters in groups of two, three, or four. That way, people have time to understand the letters or to write them.

Example: Richardson   RICH-ARD-SON

You should also pause after each syllable (each part of the word that contains a vowel sound). For example, the name Soto is SO-TO. It is helpful if you repeat your name once or twice slowly. Listen to these examples:

| Juarez | JUA-REZ | Yukari | YU-KA-RI |
| Saeed | SA-EED | Hodgkinson | HODG-KIN-SON |

B. Where do the pauses go in the spelling of these names?

Example: PE/TER CUS/TER

1. KI/MI/O TA/NA/KA
2. MI/CHA/EL CI/MI/NO
3. HIL/DA FER/RER
4. JA/MAL|THOMP/SON/

Now practice spelling these names. Remember to pause after each syllable. Practice saying the names with a classmate.

C. When saying your telephone number, your voice goes up on the third number. You also need to pause. If there is a country or an area or city code, your voice goes up on the code numbers and then you pause. Your voice goes down on the last number in the end group. Listen to these examples:

735-4024   44 (212) 988-6100

D. How do you say these numbers? Draw lines to show where your voice goes up.

Example: 626-4320

1. 938-8557
2. 001 44 352-4611
3. (941) 722-4703
4. 572 88-9740

Now practice saying these numbers with a classmate.

E. Work with a classmate. Spell your first and last names to him or her. Remember to break your name into syllables. Tell your classmate your phone number. Remember to make your voice go up and down.

5

CHALLENGE

Interview your classmates and collect as many answers as you can. Write each person's first name and a detail.

Example:

Find someone who ...	NAME	DETAIL
has an *m* in his or her last name.	*Hwa-Jeong*	*Lim*
doesn't like to talk on the phone.	*Mei-Ling*	*hates it*

Example questions:

Excuse me. How do you spell your last name?
Do you like talking on a cell phone?

Find someone who ...	NAME	DETAIL
1. has an *i* in his or her last name.	Iris	Rios
2. has a 0 in his or her phone number.		
3. has two of the same letters in his or her last name.	Eunju	898-3969
4. has a phone number with three numbers that are the same.	Eunju	898 - 3969
5. has fewer than four letters in his or her last name.		
6. has made a phone call to another country this month.		
7. has an *s* in his or her first name.		
8. has a first name that is the same length as his or her phone number.		
9. has a telephone in his or her bedroom.		
10. talks on a cellular phone often.	Joey	Yes

(handwritten: stript)   *(handwritten: FARHAT   great wall   1982)*

Listen and repeat.

What does he look like?	He has brown hair and blue eyes.
How tall is he?	He's quite tall. *(very)*
What's he like?	He's really funny.

(handwritten: pickpocket : نشّال)   *(handwritten: send)*

CONVERSATION

Listen and practice.

Jody: Hi, Tina. How was your date with Paul?
Tina: Oh, it was good, thanks.
Jody: What's he like?
Tina: Well, at first I thought he was a little serious, but he's actually really funny.
Jody: Yeah? Where did you guys go?
Tina: First we had dinner and then we went bowling. We had a great time.
Jody: Sounds good! So what does he look like?
Tina: He's quite tall, and he has curly brown hair. And he's got beautiful blue eyes!
Jody: Wow! When can I meet this guy?

(handwritten: bangs = غُرّة)   *(handwritten: bushy : كثيف)*   *(handwritten: no beard + no mustache = clean - shaven.)*

PRACTICE

Circle all the words that describe you. Tell your classmate about yourself.

Hair	Eyes	Height and weight	Personality	Other
straight	brown	short	shy	(have a) beard *(barbe)*
black *head*	blue	thin/slender	friendly	(have a) mustache
wavy	green	average weight and height	serious	(be) bald أصلع
brown	gray		sweet	(wear) glasses
curly		*heavy*	quiet	*a bald spot (petronic)*
blond		*overweight*	outgoing ≠ shy.	
long		*Tall*	funny	
red *head*		*light*	talkative	
short				
gray				

(handwritten: me)   *(handwritten: he is brunette)*   *(handwritten: She is)*   *(handwritten: He is)*

(handwritten: talks a lot easy going : relaxed (no problem) ≠ nervous, anxious.)

(handwritten: hazel eyes = blue + green)

(handwritten: chin = ذقن)   *(handwritten: أشفر = d-y-e)*
(handwritten: dimples = غمّازة)

LISTEN

Listen. Underline the correct answers to the questions you hear.

1. Q: _what does your Teacher look like?_ ?
   A: a. She's tall and thin.
      b. She's quiet and serious.

2. Q: _what color is his hair?_ ?
   A: a. It's brown.
      b. They're green.

3. Q: _what do you look like?_ ?
   A: a. I'm short and a little heavy, and I wear glasses.
      b. I'm outgoing and pretty friendly.

4. Q: _How tall are you?_ ?
   A: a. I'm 180 cm.
      b. I'm 27.

5. Q: _what color are your eyes_ ?
   A: a. I'm bald.
      b. They're blue.

6. Q: _who do you look like? your mother or your Father?_ ?
   A: a. I look like my mother.
      b. I'm like my father. _personality_

7. Q: _How old are you?_ ?
   A: a. I don't know.
      b. That's a very personal question!

8. Q: _who are you like? your mother or your Father?_ ?
   A: a. I'm like my father. He's shy and quiet, too.
      b. I look like my father. He has curly hair, too.

LISTEN AND UNDERSTAND

Listen again and write the questions. Then listen and check your answers.

8

Look at these pictures. Student B has the same pictures but in a different order. Choose a picture, but don't tell Student B who it is. Student B will ask questions and try to guess the person. You can only say "yes" or "no." Take turns asking and answering questions.

Student B: Does your person have blond hair?
Student A: No.

Student B: Is your person young?
Student A: Yes.

John

May

Andy

Judy

Jason

William

Alison

Chuck

Jean

Elizabeth

Brad

Oliver

Cynthia

Gordon

Janice

Joseph

PAIRWORK
STUDENT B

Look at these pictures. Student A has the same pictures but in a different order. Student A will choose a picture. You will ask questions and try to guess the person. Student A can only say "yes" or "no." Take turns asking and answering questions.

Student B: Does your person have blond hair?
Student A: No.

Student B: Is your person young?
Student A: Yes.

brown

Blond

Judy

Alison

Brad

Oliver

Joseph

Janice

Elizabeth

John

Chuck

May

Gordon

William

Jean

Cynthia

Andy

Jason

PRONUNCIATION

A. There are many pairs of letters that are easily confused in English. You need to be able to recognize the difference between the two sounds when you hear them. You also need to know how to make different sounds so that other people don't misunderstand you when you speak.

One pair of consonants that learners have trouble with is *l* and *r*. Listen to these examples:

lay	ray
fly	fry
glass	grass
fear	feel

The main difference between *l* and *r* is where you place your tongue. With *l*, your tongue touches the top of your mouth behind your teeth. With *r*, the tip of your tongue doesn't touch anything. But the sides of your tongue touch your back teeth.

B. Listen. Circle the words you hear.

1. Did the teacher collect / correct the homework?
2. I think this is wrong / long.
3. Let me put that on my list / wrist.
4. Did you tell Eileen / Irene?
5. Do you want the lead / red one?

C. Work with a classmate. Take turns asking and answering these questions. Find the answers in the pictures.

1. **A:** What color hair does Lisa have?
   B: _____

2. **B:** What can you say about Rob's height?
   A: _____

3. **A:** Does Rita have brown or blue eyes?
   B: _____

4. **B:** Is Alex's hair straight or curly?
   A: _____

Lisa

Rob

Rita

Alex

11

CHALLENGE

A. Mina is a member of a dating club. Read her description.

I'm average height and slender, with big, dark brown eyes. I have beautiful, long black hair. My hair is my best feature. I'm very outgoing with my friends, but a little shy with people I don't know. People say I'm a lot of fun to be with. I love sports and stay very active.

Youn Sok and Amy are lonely. They are going to join the dating club. Work in small groups and help them with their descriptions. Write about their physical characteristics and their personalities.

Youn Sok

_____
_____
_____
_____
_____
_____
_____
_____

Amy

_____
_____
_____
_____
_____
_____
_____
_____

B. Decide which group has the best description.

So, how old are you?

I'd rather not say.

Did You Know?

Asking about age and weight can be impolite. If someone asks you, and you don't want to answer, you can say, "I'd rather not say."

In the U.S. and Canada, the darkest eye color is brown. You get a "black eye" if someone hits you in the face!

sherbet

dagwood sandwich = sandwich with everything

Listen and repeat.

Are you ready to order?	I'll have the shrimp.
What kind of dressing would you like on your salad?	I think I'll have Russian.
Anything to drink?	A diet cola, please.
What did you decide on for dessert?	I'd like some ice cream.

CONVERSATION

Listen and practice.

Server: Are you ready to order?

Nick: I think so. I'll have *the fried shrimp with a baked potato and a salad.*

Server: What kind of dressing would you like on your salad?

Nick: I think I'll have *Italian*. No, make that *Russian*.

Server: Anything to drink?

Nick: *Iced tea.*

Server: And what would you like?

Beth: I'd like *a cup of vegetable soup and the chicken fajitas – with lots of onions.*

Server: Anything else?

Beth: *A diet cola*, please.

Server: What did you decide on for dessert? The *chocolate cake* is excellent!

Beth: That sounds good, but I think I'll have *a piece of apple pie with vanilla ice cream.*

Nick: Just *an espresso* for me, please.

PRACTICE

Practice the conversation above in groups of three. Choose from the foods on the menu.

Copper Kettle Café

Sandwiches
chicken mayonnaise, tuna, ham and cheese

Soup
tomato, cream of mushroom, vegetable

Salad
garden, Greek, Caesar
(salad dressings: Italian, French, Thousand Island)

Dessert
ice-cream, cheese cake, tiramisu

Tea / Coffee / Fresh orange juice

LISTEN

Look quickly at the menu. Do you know all these foods? Listen and check (✔) the foods these people order.

Today's Special

Chef's salad /Roast turkey with green beans and mashed potatoes/Cherry pie

Soups & Salads
(salad dressings: ranch, Italian, French, Russian, honey mustard, oil, vinegar)

Chicken noodle soup	cup $1.75	bowl $2.75
Cream of mushroom	cup $2.25	bowl $3.75
Chef's salad	$5.75	
Fruit salad	$6.25	
Small dinner salad	$1.50	

Sandwiches
(served on your choice of white, wheat, or rye bread)

Ham and cheese	$3.75
Tuna salad	$3.50
Pop's Burger	$3.25
Steak sandwich	$4.25

Main Courses
(include green beans and mashed potatoes)

Mom's meatloaf	$6.25
Crispy fried shrimp	$9.50
Roast turkey	$7.50
Baked chicken	$6.25
Grilled pork chops	$6.75

Desserts

Jello	$1.50
Low fat rice pudding	$1.75
Chocolate cake	$2.75
Apple pie	$2.25

Beverages

Milk	$1.25
Coffee	$1.00
Tea	$1.00
Cola	$1.00

LISTEN AND UNDERSTAND

Listen to people talking in a restaurant. Circle the correct answers.

Conversation 1

1. _____ people are going to sit together.
   a. Four
   b. Five

2. They want to sit in the _____ section.
   a. smoking
   b. non-smoking

3. They sit in the _____ section.
   a. smoking
   b. non-smoking

4. They _____ their table.
   a. like
   b. don't like

5. The table is _____ the kitchen.
   a. near
   b. away from

Conversation 2

1. The man orders _____ .
   a. beef stew
   b. a steak

2. He also asks for _____ .
   a. vegetables and french fries
   b. pasta and a salad

3. The woman says she _____ very hungry.
   a. is
   b. isn't

4. She wants a cup of _____ .
   a. coffee
   b. hot tea

5. She asks for _____ .
   a. a piece of chocolate cake
   b. a bowl of chocolate ice cream

How many are in un party? le nib

A. You are a customer in a restaurant. Student B is the server. Practice the conversation using the language in the customer boxes. Fill in the blanks with your own information. Look at the menu on page 14 if you need help. Student B begins the conversation.

Server

Customer

I'd like _____ .

I'll have _____ .

Can I have _____ ?

Server

Customer

Then I'll have _____ .

Then can I have _____ ?

Then I'd like _____ .

Server

Customer

_____ , please.

How about _____ ?

I'll have _____ .

Server

Customer

No, thanks. Just the check, please.

I don't think I want any, thanks.

Yes, I'll have _____ .

Server

B. Practice the conversation again. Order different things and use different language.

C. Now look at Student B's page. Practice the conversation again. This time, you are the server.

15

PAIRWORK
STUDENT B

A. You are a server in a restaurant. Student A is the customer. Practice the conversation using the language in the server boxes. Fill in the blanks with your own information. Look at the menu on page 14 if you need help. You begin the conversation.

Server

Are you ready to order?

Can I help you?

What would you like?

Customer

Server

I'm sorry. We don't have any _____ today.

I'm sorry. We're out of _____ .

Oh, sorry. There's/There are no _____ left.

Customer

Server

And would you like anything to drink?

And what can I get you to drink?

And what would you like to drink?

Customer

Server

What about some dessert?

Would you like anything for dessert?

Can I get you anything for dessert?

Customer

Server

OK.

Certainly.

I'll get it right away.

B. Practice the conversation again. Order different things and use different language.

C. Now look at Student A's page. Practice the conversation again. This time, you are the customer.

PRONUNCIATION

A. In Unit 2, you practiced the difference between the *l* and *r* sounds. Now try the difference between *sh* and *ch*. They are similar, so it can be difficult to hear the difference or pronounce them clearly. Listen to these examples:

shoes	choose
washes	watches
dish	ditch
shop	chop

B. **Listen. Circle the words you hear.**

1. What did you wash / watch last night?
2. There's a ship / chip in this glass.
3. Is our server's name Sherry / Cherry?
4. That shop / chop smells delicious.
5. What's in that dish / ditch?

C. To pronounce *sh*, say *s* and then move your tongue back a little. That way, more air can come out. To pronounce *ch*, say *t* and then *sh*. With *sh*, the air continues. With *ch*, the air stops.

Practice this short conversation with a classmate. Use different foods each time.

A: What would you like for a snack?

B: How about _____ ?

a chicken sandwich

some chocolate ice cream

some cheese and crackers

some French fries

a shrimp salad with Russian dressing

some fish and chips

some sugar cookies

CHALLENGE

Emca Sour food.

A. Work with a classmate. Match each dish with its country.

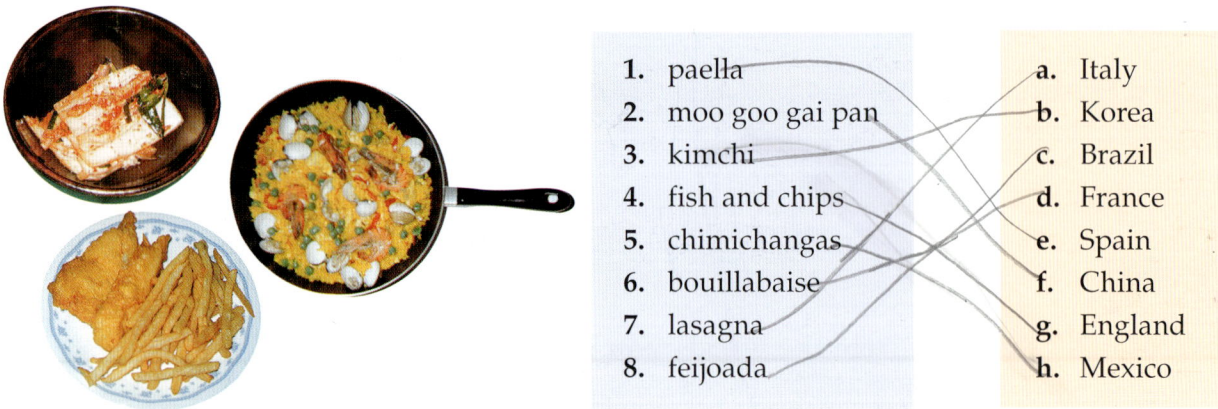

1.	paella	a. Italy
2.	moo goo gai pan	b. Korea
3.	kimchi	c. Brazil
4.	fish and chips	d. France
5.	chimichangas	e. Spain
6.	bouillabaise	f. China
7.	lasagna	g. England
8.	feijoada	h. Mexico

Do you know the name of any other dishes from these countries?

Cerelac

B. In groups of three or four, plan a trip to a local restaurant. What kind of food do you want to eat? How much do you want to spend?

C. In the U.S. and Canada, customers in restaurants usually leave the server a tip. The tip is 10–20% of the total check if they like the service.

Look at these two checks. First, add up the totals—including tax. Then figure out the tips. (The service at Coney Island Grill was OK; the service at Mario's was excellent.)

CONEY ISLAND GRILL

1 burger	4.95
1 fries	1.00
1 coffee	0.95
Tax (8.1%)	
Total	
Tip	

MARIO'S

1 shrimp cocktail	5.00
1 cup of soup	3.50
1 filet mignon	18.00
1 chicken parmagiana	14.00
2 glasses of wine	8.50
1 caesar salad	4.50
1 peach pie	3.50
1 strawberry ice cream	3.00
1 coffee	1.60
1 tea	1.60
Tax (6%)	
Total	
Tip	

Listen and repeat.

That dress looks great on you.	I look too fat.
How about this one?	Stripes make me look like a zebra.
Is there anything here you like?	That tie would look great.

CONVERSATION

Listen and practice.

Dave:	That dress looks great on you.
Marnie:	No, I think I look too fat.
Dave:	I disagree, but how about this one?
Marnie:	No, stripes make me look like a zebra.
Dave:	How about this one?
Marnie:	Are you kidding? I look like my mother.
Dave:	Here's a very nice silk outfit.
Marnie:	It's too formal.
Dave:	Is there anything here you like?
Marnie:	That tie! That tie would look great.
Dave:	Are you crazy?
Marnie:	Not for me. For you!
Dave:	I give up!

PRACTICE

Look at the words in the boxes. Ask your classmates about any words that you don't know.

Clothing items		
T-shirt	sweatshirt	blouse
shirt	turtleneck	sweater
vest	jeans	pants
shorts	dress	skirt
suit	jacket	tie
belt	socks	tights
loafers	heels	running shoes
boots	sandals	necklace
bracelet	ring	earrings

Clothing adjectives	
short-sleeved	long-sleeved
sleeveless	striped
plain	polka-dot
print	plaid
cotton	wool
denim	silk
polyester	leather

Circle the items and adjectives that describe what you are wearing today.
Describe what you are wearing to a classmate.

Example: I'm wearing a short-sleeved silk blouse and a print skirt.

LISTEN

Some people are shopping. Circle the pictures of what they are talking about.

1. a. *sneakers*    b.    c. *loafers*

2. a.    b.    c.

3. a.    b.    c.

4. a.    b.    c.

5. a. 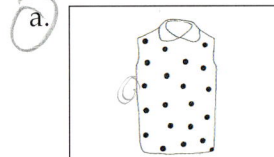   b. *shirt / ? *    c. *blouse*

6. a.    b. 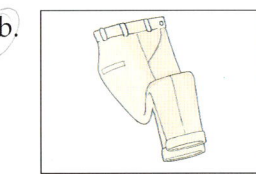 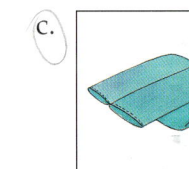   c.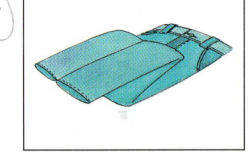

7. a.    b.    c.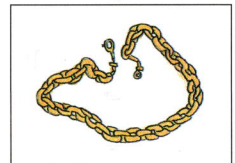

8. a.    b.    c.

Can you name all the items above?

PAIRWORK
STUDENT A

Both you and Student B have similar pictures of people in a department store. Ask and answer questions to find what is different. Write the differences below.

Example: **You:**   Is Hiro looking at a solid yellow tie?
              Student B: No. He's looking at a yellow and blue striped tie.

DIFFERENCES

In my picture:

1. _Hiro's looking at a solid yellow tie._
2. _____
3. _____
4. _____
5. _____
6. _____
7. _____
8. _____
9. _____
10. _____
11. _____
12. _____

PAIRWORK
STUDENT B

Both you and Student A have similar pictures of people in a department store. Ask and answer questions to find what is different. Write the differences below.

Example: Student A: Is Hiro looking at a solid yellow tie?
You: No. He's looking at a yellow and blue striped tie.

DIFFERENCES

In my picture:

1. <u>Hiro's looking at a yellow and blue striped tie.</u>
2. _____
3. _____
4. _____
5. _____
6. _____
7. _____
8. _____
9. _____
10. _____
11. _____
12. _____

PRONUNCIATION

A. The -*s* ending on plural nouns has three different pronunciations: *iz*, *s*, and *z*. The sound *iz* comes after the sounds *s*, *z*, *sh*, *ch*, *j*, and *zh*. Listen to these examples:

necklace	necklaces
size	sizes
brush	brushes
watch	watches

The sound *s* comes after the voiceless consonants such as *p*, *t*, *k*, and *f*. Listen to these examples:

stripe	stripes
jacket	jackets
skirt	skirts

The sound *z* comes after voiced sounds and vowels such as *b*, *d*, *g*, *m*, *r*, *l*, *a*, and *u*. Listen to these examples:

sweater	sweaters
earring	earrings
sandal	sandals

B. Listen to these words. Write them under the correct ending.

boots	shoes	purses	tights	ties	sleeves
socks	sweatshirts	pajamas	dresses	blouses	sandals

	(*iz*)	(*s*)	(*z*)
1.	purses	boots	shoes
2.	blouses	socks	pajamas
3.	dresses	swits hirts	ties
4.		tights	skeeves
			sandals

C. Practice this conversation with a classmate. Look at the pictures to decide what you are going to buy.

A: May I help you?

B: I need to buy some _____ .

A: How many pairs of _____ do you need?

B: I need _____ pair(s) of _____ .

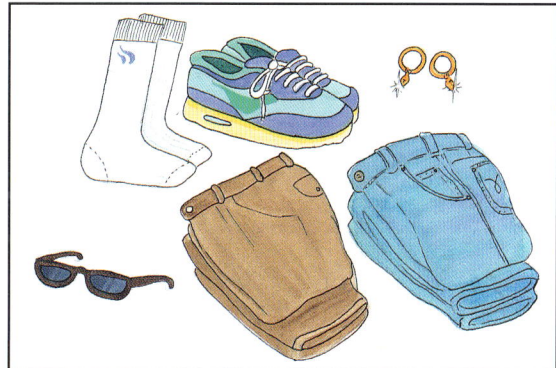

23

CHALLENGE

singular
song

A. Write your answers for questions 1–10 below. Then get two classmates'
   opinions about each store. Talk to as many different classmates as you
   can.

What is the best store for ...?	YOU	CLASSMATE #1	CLASSMATE #2
1. women's clothes			
2. men's clothes			
3. children's clothes			
4. brand name clothes			
5. athletic clothes			
6. jeans			
7. shoes			
8. jewelry			
9. sunglasses			
10. sales			

B. Work in small groups. Make a list of the most popular answers.

terrific : v. much
cer v. wonderful /good.
≠ terrible = v. bad. قبيح
Past
moving
move

Listen and repeat.

How was your weekend?	It was kind of boring.
What did you do?	I cleaned my apartment.
That's too bad.	What did you do?
I went to a soccer game.	That sounds like fun.

CONVERSATION

Listen and practice.

Toni: Hi, Luisa! How was your weekend? *little bit*

Luisa: It was kind of boring. All I did was *clean my apartment and study.*

Toni: That's too bad.

Luisa: How was yours? *v. wonderful*

Toni: I had a terrific weekend.

Luisa: I'm glad to hear that. What did you do? *whari dju do?*

Toni: Well, I *went to dinner and a movie with friends.*

Luisa: That sounds like fun.

Toni: Then on Saturday I *went skiing.* On Sunday I *slept late,* and then I *went to a soccer game with my brother.*

Luisa: You did a lot. I need to have a weekend like yours!

stop

PRACTICE

Put a check (✔) next to all the activities you did last week. Then, practice the conversation above with a classmate. Use the activities you checked.

- ☐ went for a walk
- ☑ went to a movie
- ☑ did homework
- ☑ listened to CDs
- ☐ went dancing
- ☐ bought something expensive
- ☑ watched sports on TV
- ☑ went to the library
- ☑ watched a video
- ☑ played a sport
- ☑ went to a baseball/soccer/football game

- ☑ went swimming/hiking/skiing/shopping
- ☑ worked on my computer
- ☑ cleaned my house
- ☑ visited friends/family/former classmates
- ☑ talked on the phone
- ☐ paid bills *دفع الفواتير*
- ☑ did laundry
- ☐ took care of children/baby-sat *part of it not for own baby.*
- ☑ exercised
- ☑ ate in a restaurant
- ☐ overslept/slept late

dormir beau coup
نام أكثر من اللازم، ينام كثيرا
ينام في وقت متأخر

25

LISTEN

Listen to the conversation. Then number the pictures in order from 1 to 6.

I took one sip (Liquid) فقه

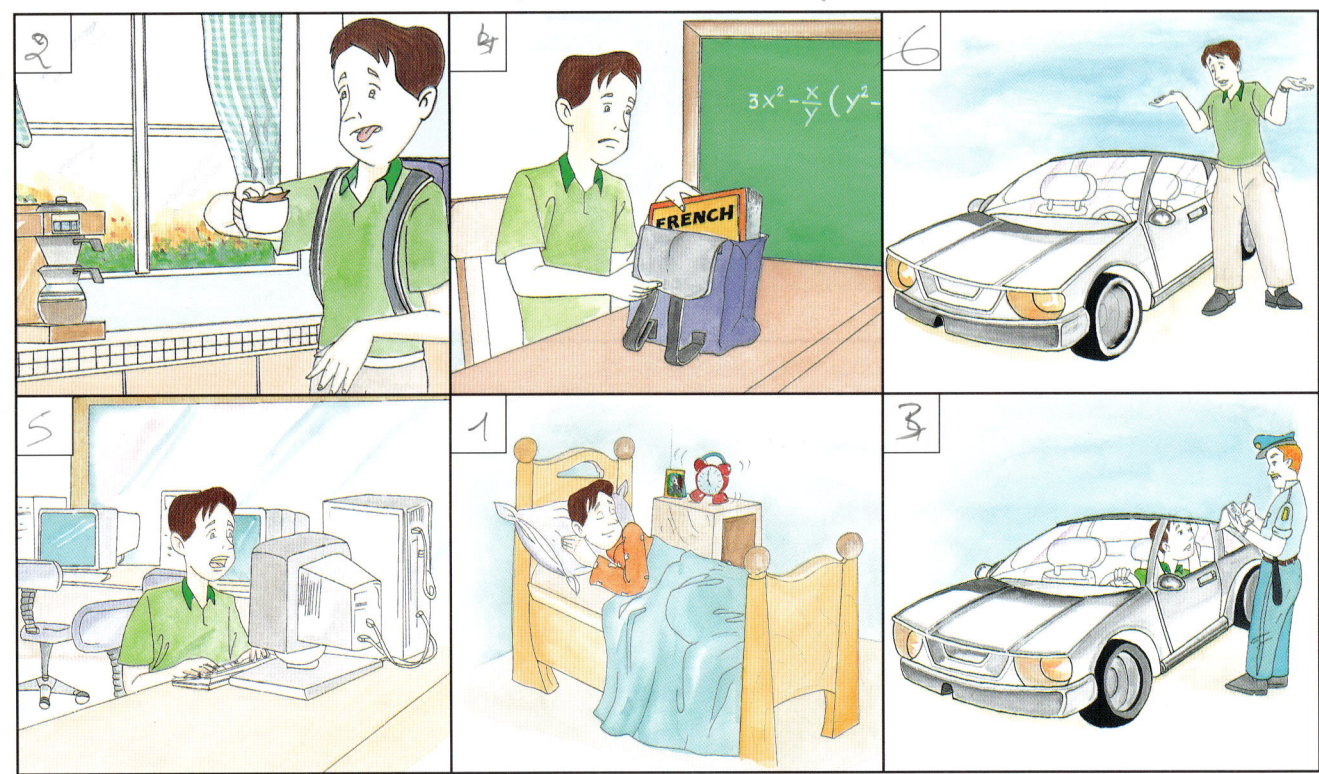

2 | 4 | 6

FRENCH

$3x^2 - \dfrac{x}{y}\,(y^2$

5 | 1 | 3

LISTEN AND UNDERSTAND

Listen again. Complete the sentences with the missing information.

Bruce …

1. over *slept* _____ .

2. drank bad ___*cream*_____ .
   Past of drink

3. _*got a*_____ a ticket.

4. _*He brought*_____ the wrong book.

5. _*He forgot*_____ to save his information.

6. _*He lost*_____ his keys.

- drink → drank
- drive → drove
- bring → brought
- sleep → slept
- get → got

forget → forgot
find → found
swim → swam
teach → taught

26

[handwritten notes in top margin: "what was open?", "except money – much: non countbl.", "many: countble (books)"]

You received a postcard from a friend. Some of the information has been erased. Ask Student B for the missing information.

Example: Where did Nina and her friends go yesterday?

Greetings from New York!

We're having a great time. Yesterday we went _to the statue of liberty_. We took a boat to get there, and then we climbed to _top of the statue_. We stayed there for about two hours. Afterwards, we walked to Chinatown and ate in a restaurant. The food was _really great_. It was cheap, too: I paid only _10 $_ for the meal! At night, we saw a Broadway show. It was _good_, but our seats were at the _back of the theatre_, so we couldn't see or hear very well. Broadway was crowded, and a lot of stores were open. I bought _2 CDs and a sweatshirt_. By the time we went to bed at 1:00 a.m., we were really tired. Anyway, today we're going to museums.

　　See you soon,
　　Nina

[handwritten: "you look sleepy"]

missed

PAIRWORK
STUDENT B

You received a postcard from a friend. Some of the information has been erased. Ask Student A for the missing information.

Example: How did Nina and her friends get to the Statue of Liberty?

> Greetings from New York!
> We're having a great time. Yesterday we went to the Statue of Liberty. We _____ to get there, and then we climbed to the top of the statue. We stayed there for _____ . Afterwards, we walked to _____ and _____ . The food was really great. It was cheap, too: I paid only ten dollars for the meal! At night, we saw _____ . It was good, but our seats were at the back of the theater, so we couldn't see or hear very well. Broadway was crowded, and _____ were open. I bought two CDs and a sweatshirt. By the time we went to bed at_____ a.m., we were really tired. Anyway, today we're going to museums.
>
> See you soon,
> Nina

USA 32

467521

PRONUNCIATION

defin : يعرف
smooth : يمهد

A. The *-ed* ending on regular verbs in the simple past tense has three different pronunciations: *id, t* and *d*.

The *id* ending is the easiest to learn: it is pronounced after *t* and *d*. Listen to these examples:

want	wanted
add	added
rent	rented
visit	visited

toot   tooted

depended
collide → collided

→ *valueless.*

The sound *t* is pronounced after the sounds *f, k, p, s, t, ch,* and *sh*. Listen to these examples:

laugh	laughed
like	liked
watch	watched
wash	washed

miss   missed.

liked /t/
talk : /talkt/
sip → sipped /t/   th
wish → wished /t/

The *d* ending is pronounced after the sounds *b, v, g, j, l, r, m, n,* and *ng*. Listen to these examples:

call	called
live	lived
listen	listened
stay	stayed

mime   mimed

answer → answered /ʋ/ a b sound
th ≈ → smooth → smoothed

B. Listen to these verbs. Write them under the correct ending.

missed	added	kissed	helped	practiced	rented
exercised	cried	wanted	started	called	used

(t)	*(d)*	*(id)*
missed	exercised	added
kissed	cried	wanted
helped	called	started
practiced	used	rented

C. Practice these short conversations with a classmate. Use the verbs in the box.

watch *t*	talk *t*	listen *d*	wash
study *id*	work *t*	call *d*	stay

1. **A:** What did you do last night?

    B: _____ .

2. **A:** What did you do last weekend?

    B: _____ .

29

CHALLENGE

A. Masato had a dream last night but he can't remember it very well. He thinks it was a good dream, but he's not sure. Work in small groups. Choose some of the pictures below and create a dream for Masato.

Tell Masato's dream to the other groups.

B. Write Masato's dream below.

_____

_____

_____

_____

_____

_____

_____

_____

_____

Present

Listen and repeat.

We've got a lot of problems.   What's wrong?
The sink is stopped up.   I'll call the plumber.
And the dog is sick.   I'll call the vet.
There's something else. The car won't start.   What else is going to go wrong?

CONVERSATION

Listen and practice.

Craig: Mom, we've got a lot of problems here!
Mother: What's wrong?
Craig: There's a problem with the sink.
Mother: What?
Craig: It's stopped up again.
Mother: I'll call the plumber. What's that noise?
Craig: That's Rex. He's sick.
Mother: Oh, no. I'll call the vet.
Craig: There's something else. The car won't start.
Mother: Good grief! What else is going to go wrong today?

won't

plumber
electrician
vet
mechanic
manger

PRACTICE

Who'll fix the problem? Match the problem with a person.

1. The music is too loud.
2. The light won't turn on.
3. The car battery is dead.
5. The cat won't eat.
5. The sink is stopped up.
6. My back went out. I can't walk.

5. plumber
2. electrician
6. doctor
3. mechanic
1. manager
4. vet

*stopped
dead*

Choose a problem. Say it to a classmate. He or she will answer:

I'll call the _____ .

LISTEN

Listen and look at the pictures. Write the responses you hear under the pictures.

1.

I'll get it.

2.

I'll explain it to you.

3.

I'll dry

4.

I'll check the Battery

5.

I'll turn it down

6.

I'll call the doctor

LISTEN AND UNDERSTAND

Listen to the conversation. Circle the best answers.

1. Who are the speakers?
   a. friends
   b. classmates
   c. boyfriend-girlfriend

2. What does Julie say about the class?
   a. It's easy now.
   b. It will be harder later.
   c. It's difficult for her.

3. What are the speakers going to do?
   a. Have coffee and then study.
   b. Go to a biology class.
   c. Meet on Friday to study.

4. Who will pay for the coffee?
   a. He will.
   b. She will.
   c. They will each pay for their own.

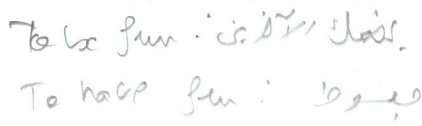

A. **Look at the chart. There are six people. One of them has these plans:**

> Ten years from now, I am going to be married. I am going to be the head of a big company. I am going to be very rich. I am going to own a Rolls Royce and a big house near the sea. I think I will be very happy.
> Who am I?

Student B has the answer. Ask Student B questions and fill in the chart. Student B can only answer "yes" or "no."

Example: **Student A:** Is Jeffrey going to be married?
          Student B: Yes.

	married	head of co.	rich	Rolls Royce	big house
Jeffrey	yes				
Alison		no			
Mariah			yes		
Mitch				yes	
Theo					yes

B. **Now Student B will ask you questions. You have the answers. Look at the chart and answer Student B's questions. You can only say "yes" or "no."**

> Here are my plans. 10 years from now, I am going to be single. I am going to work very hard. I am going to have a lot of money, but I am going to give most of my money away to other people. I am going to live a simple life. I think I am going to be very happy.
> Who am I?

	single	work hard	a lot of money	give money away	simple life
Pamela	yes	yes	yes	no	yes
Joseph	yes	yes	yes	no	no
Mark	yes	yes	yes	yes	yes
Cary	yes	no	yes	yes	yes
Ross	no	yes	yes	yes	yes

Which person do you think will be happier? Why?

33

PAIRWORK
STUDENT B

A. **Look at the chart. There are six people. One of them has these plans:**

> Ten years from now, I am going to be married. I am going to be the head of a big company. I am going to be very rich. I am going to own a Rolls Royce and a big house near the sea. I think I will be very happy.
>   Who am I?

You have the answer. Student A will ask you questions. Look at the chart and answer Student A's questions. You can only say "yes" or "no."

Example: Student A: Is Jeffrey going to be married?
              Student B: Yes.

	married	head of co.	rich	Rolls Royce	big house
Jeffrey	yes	yes	yes	no	no
Alison	yes	no	yes	no	yes
Mariah	yes	no	yes	yes	yes
Mitch	no	yes	yes	yes	yes
Theo	yes	yes	yes	yes	yes

B. **Now Student A has the answers. Ask Student A questions and fill in the chart. Student A can only answer "yes" or "no."**

> Here are my plans. 10 years from now, I am going to be single. I am going to work very hard. I am going to have a lot of money, but I am going to give most of my money away to other people. I am going to live a simple life. I think I am going to be very happy.
>   Who am I?

	single	work hard	a lot of money	give money away	simple life
Pamela	yes				
Joseph		yes			
Mark			yes		
Cary				yes	
Ross					yes

Which person do you think will be happier? Why?

PRONUNCIATION

Dictation

going to = gonna

A. *Going to* is often pronounced *gonna*. Listen to these examples:

wharaya

> **A:** What are you going to (*gonna*) do tonight?
> **B:** We're going to (*gonna*) see a movie.

B. Listen and complete the sentences below.

1. They _'re going to be_ late for the party.
2. Who's _going to wash_ the dishes?
3. I'm _going to do_ my homework now.
4. She's _going to get_ some fast food.
5. What _are you going to do_?

C. In spoken English, *will* is used in the contracted form (*I'll, you'll, he'll, she'll*, etc.). Listen to these examples.

will

> I'll be home tonight.
> You'll feel better tomorrow.
> He'll come to class next week.
> She'll help you.
>
> It'll rain tomorrow.
> We'll see you later.
> They'll call this weekend.

Jenny 'll

D. Listen to these sentences. Fill in the blanks with the correct contraction.

1. _They'll_ tell me later.
2. _they'll_ meet us after the soccer game.
3. _I'll_ stop by in the morning.
4. _He'll_ try to help you.
5. _they'll_ call in a few minutes.

E. Practice these conversations with a classmate. Use information about yourself.

1. **A:** What are you going to do this weekend?

   B: I'm going to _____ . How about you?

   A: I'm going to _____ .

2. **A:** When will you _____ ?

   B: I'll _____ . What about you?

   A: I'll _____ .

CHALLENGE

Lee, Linda, Larry, Lance, Lesley, Logan, and Laura all work in an office together. They are talking about their futures. Two of them are getting married soon, but it's a secret. They are not telling anyone. Who will be the married couple? Work in small groups. First read their statements and then read the other information. Decide who the married couple will be.

Statements

1. Lee: "I'm going to go on an African safari for vacation. I will definitely go alone. I prefer to be alone."
2. Lance: "I will never tell you what I plan to do. I like to keep secrets."
3. Linda: "I'm going to marry my best friend."
4. Larry: "Lance is lying. He told me he's going to do something special next month."
5. Lesley: "A career is more important to me than marriage."
6. Laura: "I won't be happy until I am married."
7. Logan: "When I was a child, Linda and I spent a lot of time together. I think we're going to be friends the rest of our lives."

Other information

1. Larry is lying.
2. Lance is going to a jewelry store tomorrow.
3. Logan never wears his wedding ring. It's uncomfortable.
4. Linda's boyfriend wants her to change jobs. His company pays better.
5. Lesley is going to quit work soon. She will be the first person to leave the company.
6. Larry is an only child.
7. Lee doesn't have a girlfriend.
8. After next week, Laura and Lance aren't going to work in the same department.
9. Larry's parents don't like their daughter-in-law.
10. The president of the company is upset that his girlfriend is going to leave the company.

Listen and repeat.

When will she be back?	The day after tomorrow.
What day is it?	It's the 3rd of January.
When's your baby due?	A month from now.

(handwritten: centuries : القرون)
(handwritten above 3rd: Thourd)

CONVERSATIONS

Listen and practice.

A. **Bonnie:** Did you call Jan?
   Mark: Yes. The day before yesterday.
   Bonnie: What did she say? Is she engaged?
   Mark: She won't be home until the day after tomorrow.
   Bonnie: I really wanted to know!
   Mark: Why don't you call her when she gets back?
   Bonnie: I don't like to ask personal questions!
   Mark: But it's OK if I do, right?

B. **Rita:** So when's your baby due? → *scheduled, expect موعد ولادة (airplane)*
   Lynn: A month from now.
   Rita: Next month? You're kidding. That's so soon.
   Lynn: Not for me. I'm ready right now. *informal : I'm sure of this) 90% certain)*
   Rita: I bet. *formal (to gamble) يراهن*

(handwritten: yesterday morning / " afternoon / last night (Yesterday, night))

PRACTICE

Look at the calendar and answer the questions.
Today is Monday, the 14th.

1. The day before yesterday was __Saturday 12th__.
2. Three days ago was __Friday 11th__.
3. The day after next is __Wednesday 16th__.
4. The day before last was __Saturday 12th__.
5. A week ago Sunday was __sixth__.
6. Two days from now is __Wednesday 16th__.

DECEMBER

S	M	T	W	Th	F	S
		1	2	3	4	5
6	7	8	9	10	11	12
13	(14)	15	16	17	18	19
20	21	22	23	24	25	26
27	28	29	30	31		

LISTEN

Listen. **Match the numbers of the sentences to the dates below.**

20th	_8_	21st	_1_
1st	_3_	12th	_2_
3rd	_11_	30th	_10_
13th	_5_	8th	_5_
5th	_6_	10th	_7_
2nd	_9_	11th	_12_

LISTEN AND UNDERSTAND

Listen to the conversation and look at the calendar.
Write the dates for 1–5 below.

Today is the 13th.

1. car accident — Tues 10th
2. insurance canceled — Monday 9th
3. girlfriend's letter — Wed 11th
4. girlfriend's visit — Fri 20th
5. girlfriend's birthday — Sund 15th

Sunday	Monday	Tuesday	Wednesday	Thursday	Friday	Saturday
1	2	3	4	5	6	7
8	9	10	11	12	13	14
15	16	17	18	19	20	21
22	23	24	25	26	27	28
29	30					

A. Student B is going to tell you about Ben's exciting month. Write the date for each event. Then check with Student B and see if you have the same dates.

Sunday	Monday	Tuesday	Wednesday	Thursday	Friday	Saturday
		1	2	3	4	5
6	7	8	9	10	11	12
13	14	15	16	17	18	19
20	21	22	23	24	25	26
27	28	29	30	31		

Today is the 2nd.

a. get married _____

b. honeymoon _____

c. a new job _____

d. move house _____

e. graduate _____

f. a new car _____

B. Now you will tell Student B about Susan's busy month. Student B will write the dates. You can only use time phrases, not numbers, to give the information, for example: *two days ago, a week ago Monday, a week ago yesterday*, etc. Then check with Student B and see if you have the same dates.

Sunday	Monday	Tuesday	Wednesday	Thursday	Friday	Saturday
	1	2	3	4	5	6
7	8	9	10	11	12	13
14	15	16	17	18	19	20
21	22	23	24	25	26	27
28	29	30	31			

Today is the 20th.

a. She had a party for 50 people on the 13th.

b. She took care of her friend's four-year-old son on the 5th.

c. She took her grandmother to the doctor on the 17th.

d. She began a karate class on the 18th.

e. She taught an aerobics class on the 15th.

f. She lost her purse on the 8th.

PAIRWORK
STUDENT B

A. You are going to tell Student A about Ben's exciting month. Student A will write the dates. You can only use time phrases, not numbers, to give the information, for example: *a week from tomorrow, two days from now, the day after next*, etc. Then check with Student A and see if you have the same dates.

Sunday	Monday	Tuesday	Wednesday	Thursday	Friday	Saturday
		1	2	3	4	5
6	7	8	9	10	11	12
13	14	15	16	17	18	19
20	21	22	23	24	25	26
27	28	29	30	31		

Today is the 2nd.

a. Ben's going to get married on the 4th.
b. He's going to Hawaii for his honeymoon on the 5th.
c. He's going to start a new job on the 23rd.
d. He's going to move house on the 15th.
e. He's going to graduate from college on the 31st.
f. He's going to get a sports car on the 26th.

B. Now Student A will tell you about Susan's busy month. Write the date for each event. Then check with Student A and see if you have the same dates.

Sunday	Monday	Tuesday	Wednesday	Thursday	Friday	Saturday
	1	2	3	4	5	6
7	8	9	10	11	12	13
14	15	16	17	18	19	20
21	22	23	24	25	26	27
28	29	30	31			

Today is the 20th.

a. party _____

b. friend's son _____

c. grandmother _____

d. karate class _____

e. aerobics class _____

f. purse _____

PRONUNCIATION

A. Numbers like *fifth* and *sixth* are good practice for the *th* sound at the end of words. Listen to these numbers:

fourth	seventh	tenth	eleventh	fifteenth

Make sure you give yourself time to make the *th* sound. Practice saying the above numbers.

B. Work with a classmate. Look at Lynn's calendar for the month of May. Take turns telling each other about Lynn's month. Today is May 12th.

Example: On May 5th, Lynn prepared food for a picnic.
On May 25th, Lynn is going to paint the kitchen.

Sunday	Monday	Tuesday	Wednesday	Thursday	Friday	Saturday
			1	2 sale at Bloomies - get new suit	3	4 tennis with Pat
5 prepare food for picnic	6 go to picnic	7	8 meet Grandma and Aunt Mae - lunch at Jackie's Place 11.30	9 meet with Ms. Williams for day care job	10 help Ricky clean house	11
12	13	14 volleyball practice	15 call Mrs. Williams - job? Y/N?	16 pick up Sam at airport 7pm	17 dinner party for Ricky, Sue, Jim and Lara	18 volleyball practice at 10am/ see dentist at 2pm
19	20 go to Ricky's party	21	22 take Mom and Dad out to anniversary dinner	23 play volleyball game 5.30	24 buy paint, ladder, etc at Homes R Us	25 paint kitchen
26 paint kitchen	27 buy birthday present for Alex	28 pay bills, balance check book	29 doctor's appointment	30 finish report	31 dinner/ theater with Ricky	

CHALLENGE

A. Work with a classmate. Read the information below, and use the calendar to solve the puzzles.

Sunday	Monday	Tuesday	Wednesday	Thursday	Friday	Saturday
			1	2	3	4
5	6	7	8	9	10	11
12	13	14	15	16	17	18
19	20	21	22	23	24	25
26	27	28	29	30	31	

1. Today is the 7th.
   a. Tom is going to the dentist the day after tomorrow.
   b. Bob is going to the dentist the day after next.
   c. Joe is going to the dentist a week from tomorrow.
   d. Bill is going to the dentist a week from next Tuesday.
   e. Sam is going to the dentist a week from Wednesday.

   Who will be at the dentist on the 21st? _____Bill_____

2. Today is the 29th.
   a. Two days ago, Sue left for Switzerland.
   b. A week ago yesterday, Jane left for Switzerland.
   c. A week ago Sunday, Kim left for Switzerland.
   d. The day before last, Kay left for Switzerland.
   e. Two weeks ago yesterday, Jill left for Switzerland.

   Who left for Switzerland on the 19th? _____Kim_____

3. Today is the 26th.
   a. A week ago Saturday, the Lims began their honeymoon.
   b. A week ago last Thursday, the Smiths began their honeymoon.
   c. The day before last, the Roses began their honeymoon.
   d. Two weeks ago yesterday, the Grays began their honeymoon.
   e. Three days ago, the Tans began their honeymoon.

   Who began their honeymoon on the 11th? _____Grays_____

B. Prepare your own puzzle and give it to your partner to solve.

Today is the _____ .

   a. _____

   b. _____

   c. _____

   d. _____

   e. _____

   _____ ?

Listen and repeat.

Smooth = لين
= no shappy تقطيع

I need to book a flight.
How may I direct your call?
Do you have anything for the 20th?
What city are you leaving from?

What day would you like to travel?
Reservations, please.
I'm sorry. Those rooms are all sold out.
Vancouver, Canada.

CONVERSATIONS

Listen and practice.

A.
Ticket Agent:	Elite Travel Agency. How may I help you?
Gina:	I need to book a flight to Hong Kong next month.
Ticket Agent:	All right. What city are you leaving from?
Gina:	Vancouver, Canada.
Ticket Agent:	What day would you like to travel?
Gina:	That depends. I'd like to get the best rate.
Ticket Agent:	That would be a Saturday or Sunday.
Gina:	OK. Let's see. How about Saturday, June 11?
Ticket Agent:	There's a flight leaving at 9 a.m., with a layover at Narita and continuing to Hong Kong three hours later.
Gina:	That sounds fine.
Ticket Agent:	Let me check what seats are available.

B.
Hotel Clerk:	Downtown Plaza Hotel. How may I direct your call?
Joseph:	Reservations, please.
Reservations:	Reservations. How may I help you?
Joseph:	This is Joseph Bradley. I have a reservation for June 15. I need to reschedule.
Reservations:	OK. When would you like to come?
Joseph:	Do you have anything for the 20th?
Reservations:	I'm sorry. There are no vacancies that night. There's a conference in town.
Joseph:	What about the 21st?
Reservations:	I have one room left in the non-smoking section.
Joseph:	That would be fine.

PRACTICE

Work with a classmate. Put the following time expressions in order.

_____ midnight   _____ 7 in the evening   _____ 4 in the afternoon

_____ 3 p.m.   _____ noon   _____ 5 p.m.

_____ 10 in the morning   *1* 8 a.m.   _____ 9 a.m.

43

LISTEN

Listen to the conversations. Circle the correct answers.

1. The appointment will be **today** tomorrow
2. The appointment will be at **8:15** 8:50
3. The appointment will be this week **next week**
4. The appointment is **canceled** rescheduled
5. The appointment will be on Saturday morning **Saturday afternoon**
6. The appointment will be on Tuesday **Thursday**

LISTEN AND UNDERSTAND

Listen to each conversation. Fill in the blanks with the information for each reservation or appointment.

	Day of the Week	AM or PM	Time
1.	Friday	PM	4:30
2.	Wednesday	AM	8:00
3.	thursday	P.M	12:0

HWK

A. You want to schedule an appointment for next week with your doctor, Dr. Kim. Student B is Dr. Kim's receptionist. First complete the calendar below with your schedule for next week. Include times for each event.

Monday	Tuesday	Wednesday	Thursday	Friday
- 8 → 12 : school - go to school from 8 → 12 am	- go shopping with friends from : 12 PM → 1 PM	- appointment with the dentist from 4 PM → 6 PM	- haircut from 8 → 8:30 pm	- drink coffee with friends from : 12:30 PM → 2 pm

Practice the conversation below with Student B, using the information in your schedule. (Note: It takes 30 minutes to get to Dr. Kim's office from your home.)

Receptionist: Dr. Kim's office. This is ___Mary___ (Student B's name).
Student A: I'd like to make an appointment with Dr. Kim.
Receptionist: OK. When would you like to come in?
Student A: Sometime next week.
Receptionist: All right. How about ___Tuesday___ (day)?

Continue the conversation. Remember to use expressions for suggesting times:

What about _____ ?

How about _____ ?

Would _____ be OK?

When you find a good appointment time, end the conversation.

B. Now look at Student B's page. Practice the conversation again. This time, you are the receptionist.

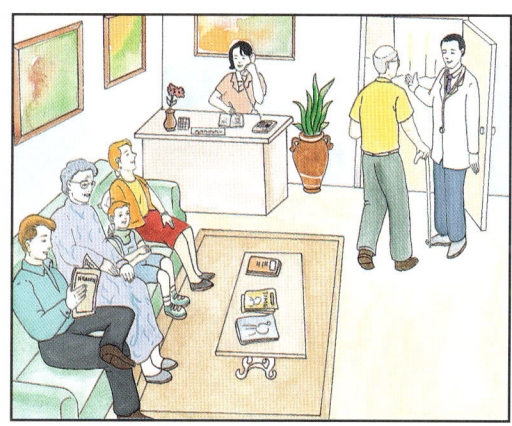

PAIRWORK
STUDENT B

A. You work as the receptionist at a doctor's office (Dr. Kim). Student A wants to make an appointment for next week. First, look at Dr. Kim's schedule for next week.

Time	Monday	Tuesday	Wednesday	Thursday	Friday
9–10	XXXXX	R. Shapiro	N. Anders		
10–11	XXXXX	M. Gomez		J. Picanti	
11–12	XXXXX	C. Boulet	E. Moi	V. Ortega	
12–2	XXXXX	XXXXX	XXXXX	XXXXX	XXXXX
2–3	T. Yamada		Y. Hung	P. Romero	XXXXX
3–4	B. Hassan	A. Ferreira		H. Jackson	XXXXX
4–5		D. Nuwad	F. Bell	XXXXX	
5–6	R. Chung	G. Thomas	XXXXX	W. Syms	XXXXX

Practice the conversation below with Student A, using the information in Dr. Kim's schedule. (Note: XXXXX means Dr. Kim won't be in the office.)

Receptionist: Dr. Kim's office. This is ____Mary____ (your name).
Student A: I'd like to make an appointment with Dr. Kim.
Receptionist: OK. When would you like to come in?
Student A: Sometime next week.
Receptionist: All right. How about _Monday 9—10_ (day)?

Continue the conversation. Remember to use expressions for suggesting times:

What about _____ ?

How about _____ ?

Would _____ be OK?

When you find a good appointment time, end the conversation.

B. Now look at Student A's page. Practice the conversation again. This time, you are the patient.

PRONUNCIATION

A. Words in English have stressed and unstressed syllables. This means that some syllables are strong and some are weak. Listen to these examples:

• ○ dentist	○ • ○ tomorrow
• ○ midnight	○ • ○ ○ receptionist

B. Listen to these words. Darken the stressed syllable.

1. ○ ○
doctor
2. ○ ○ ○ ○
reservation
3. ○ ○
cancel
4. ○ ○ ○
appointment
5. ○ ○
schedule

6. ○ ○ ○
Saturday
7. ○ ○ ○
layover
8. ○ ○ ○
afternoon
9. ○ ○ ○
Wednesday
10. ○ ○ ○
opening

C. Practice the conversation with a classmate. Use the words in the box to fill in the blanks. Pay special attention to the word stress.

A: I'd like to make a _____ reservation.

B: For what day?

A: _____

1. dinner / Saturday evening
2. lunch / Friday at noon
3. brunch / Sunday morning
4. flight / Tuesday at midnight

CHALLENGE

A. Check all of the following that are important to you when you make a reservation.

airplane	hotel	restaurant
☐ non-smoking section	☐ view	☐ window table
☐ children fly half price	☐ pets allowed	☐ corner table
☐ window/aisle seat	☐ children stay free	☐ table outdoors
☐ quick check-in	☐ 5 stars	☐ table away from kitchen
☐ frequent flyer mileage	☐ 24-hour room service	☐ smoking allowed

B. Jenny, Kenny, Lenny, and Penny are all traveling. Two are on an airplane, one is at a hotel, and one is at a restaurant. Who is where? Work in small groups.

1. The vegetarian has the aisle seat.
2. One of the travelers doesn't smoke. She won't take a smoking flight.
3. Jenny is the oldest traveler.
4. The window seat on the plane has a woman in it.
5. One of the travelers is unhappy with the room service at his hotel.
6. Kenny ordered steak for lunch.
7. The airline allows smoking.
8. Jenny has only a small bag so she can do a quick check-in.
9. The youngest person has the table with a view.

Listen and repeat.

Is this homemade?	Yes, it is.
What else does your husband do?	He makes the dinner.
Who does the cleaning?	We all do, even the kids.

CONVERSATION

Listen and practice.

Nora: This is wonderful pie. Is it homemade?
Carol: It is. But I didn't make it. Jack did.
Nora: I didn't know your husband baked.
Carol: Every week he bakes something wonderful. He makes incredible fresh bread.
Nora: What else does your amazing husband do?
Carol: He makes the dinner every night.
Nora: Really! My husband doesn't even know how to fry an egg!
Carol: Jack even does the laundry. I have a longer commute and spend fewer hours at home, so he doesn't mind.
Nora: That's wonderful. Who does the cleaning?
Carol: We both do. That way it only takes a small part of Saturday.
Nora: Carol, can I move in with you?

PRACTICE

Tell a classmate about your home life. What jobs do you do?

Who does the cleaning?	Who does the food shopping?
Who does the cooking?	Who does the laundry?
Who does the ironing?	Who does the yardwork?
Who makes the beds?	Who works the hardest in your family?
Who makes lunch?	

LISTEN

Make or *do*? Listen to the conversations. Write the correct verb.

1. _make_ bread
2. _do_ the dishes
3. _make_ dinner

    make sandwiches
4. _do_ the housework

    _do_ the vacuuming Hoover
5. _do_ the weeding
5. _do_ the homework
6. _make_ the bed

    make breakfast
7. _make_ a phone call
8. _make_ a mistake

make a speech ot
or give a "

LISTEN AND UNDERSTAND

Circle the correct verbs below. Then listen to the conversation and check your answers.

1. made (did) my make-up
2. (made) did lunch
3. made (did) the laundry
4. made (did) the ironing
5. (made) did a cake
6. (made) did a mess
7. (made) did sandwiches
8. (made) did a cup of coffee

PAIRWORK
STUDENT A

What's happening at the Park Hotel? Describe what you see with *make* and *do*.

Examples: One of the guests is making a mess.
One of the staff is making a cup of coffee.

Work with Student B. Ask questions to find these people in the picture above. Student B has the answers.

| Jody | Bill | Keiko | Sunil | Wanida | Fred |

Example: Student A: What's Jody doing?
Student B: She's doing her make-up.

Now help Student B find these people in the picture. Use *do* or *make* when you answer Student B's questions.

Craig Yong Jin Fumiko Yuri Mike Maria

PAIRWORK
STUDENT B

What's happening at the Park Hotel? Describe what you see with *make* and *do*.

Examples: One of the guests is making a mess.
One of the staff is making a cup of coffee.

Work with Student A. Help Student A find these people in the picture above. Use *do* or *make* when you answer Student A's questions.

Jody

Bill

Keiko

Sunil

Wanida

Fred

Example: **Student A:** What's Jody doing?
Student B: She's doing her make-up.

Now ask questions to find these people in the picture. Student A has the answers.

Craig   Yong Jin   Fumiko   Yuri   Mike   Maria

to make up = صورة

PRONUNCIATION

A. In English, some sentences go up at the end, and some sentences go down at the end. This is called *intonation*. Listen to these examples:

Pattern = shape

A: Do you like to clean?

B: No, I don't like to clean.

A: What do you like to do?

B: I like to relax.

Here are the two common patterns:

Pattern A

statements: I like to make dinner.

wh- questions: What do you like to make?

Pattern B

yes/no questions: Do you like to make dinner?

B. Listen to these sentences. Write if the pattern is A or B.

1. Who does the cooking in your family?   _____
2. Do you ever do the vacuuming?   _____
3. When do you do your homework?   _____
4. I always make sandwiches for lunch.   _____
5. No one in my family makes their bed.   _____

C. Practice this conversation with a classmate. Use information about yourself. Pay special attention to the intonation.

A: Do you like to _____ ?

B: No, I don't like to _____ .

A: What do you like to do?

B: I like to _____ .

Tarbouche
~~From~~ From
Lebanon

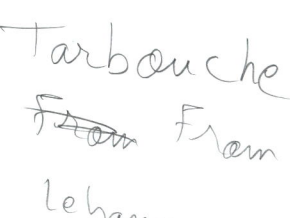

53

CHALLENGE

What should you think about when you're choosing a roommate or housemate? Circle your opinion next to each statement: 1, 2, or 3 (1 = very important, 2 = important, 3 = not important).

Roommates/housemates should …	Your opinion		
1. do their dishes right after eating.	①	②	3
X 2. make their bed every morning.	①	2	3
3. do an equal amount of housework.	①	2	3
X 4. make meals for each other.	1	2	③
X 5. socialize together.	①	2	3
6. not make phone calls after 11 p.m.	1	2	③
7. not make a lot of noise.	①	2	3
8. not make a mess.	①	2	3
9. take turns doing the laundry.	①	2	3
10. _has to be clean_ (add your own idea)	1	2	3
11. _take turns doing ironing_ (add your own idea)	1	2	3

In small groups, share your answers. How many are the same? How many are different?

Who could you share rooms with? Find another student in your group or in the class you could share a room with.

Listen and repeat.

Would you like to go to the mall with me tomorrow? Sounds good.
I need to get a new sports jacket and tie. OK, what time?
Can I pick you up around 11:30? Great. See you then.

CONVERSATION

Listen and practice.

Kate: Hello.
Jack: Kate? It's Jack.
Kate: Hi, Jack. How are you?
Jack: Great. I was wondering. Would you like to go to the mall with me tomorrow? I need to get some clothes for a wedding.
Kate: Sounds good. Who's getting married?
Jack: My friend Bob. I need to get a new sports jacket and tie.
Kate: I've never seen you wear a tie.
Jack: Well, I don't very often, but it's a wedding.
Kate: OK, what time?
Jack: Can I pick you up around 11:30? We can have lunch at the food court.
Kate: Great. Eleven thirty tomorrow, my house?
Jack: See you then.

PRACTICE

Work with a classmate. Look at the conversation. How many changes can you make in five minutes? Write them below.

Old	New
Great.	_Not too good._
_____	_____
_____	_____
_____	_____
_____	_____
_____	_____

LISTEN

Listen to the conversations. Then read the sentences. Listen again and circle the correct answers.

Conversation 1

1.	The man needs to see a dentist.	yes	no
2.	There are several openings for today.	yes	no
3.	He wants an appointment for 2:00.	yes	no
4.	The appointment is for 9:50.	yes	no

Conversation 2

1.	The man's last name is Hanson.	yes	no
2.	He lives in a house, not an apartment.	yes	no
3.	He is 17 years old.	yes	no
4.	He gives his phone number.	yes	no

Conversation 3

1.	The woman made the beds.	yes	no
2.	She will clean the house this afternoon.	yes	no
3.	The yard work is finished.	yes	no
4.	She's going to relax.	yes	no

PAIRWORK

Work with a classmate. Take turns asking and answering the questions below. Say at least three sentences in your answers.

1. What does your favorite actor look like? Don't say a name. Just tell me what the actor looks like. I'll try to guess.

2. What's your favorite place to eat lunch? Why?

3. What kind of person are you?

4. What are your favorite clothes?

5. What did you do last Saturday?

6. What's something you really do not like to do?

7. Tell me about a really good day you had.

8. What are you going to do after class?

9. What does your favorite singer look like? Don't say a name. Just tell me what the singer looks like. I'll try to guess.

10. What's your favorite restaurant? Why?

11. Describe your best friend's personality.

12. What fashions don't you like?

13. What did you do last Sunday?

14. What's something you really like to do?

15. Tell me about a really bad day you had.

16. What are you going to do next weekend?

Around Town I

 **W**ork in groups of four. Each person places a chip on START. Take turns to throw the die and move your chip. Answer the question or follow the instruction.

1 **START**	**2** Call one of the people in your group. Make plans for today. You want to go shopping.	**3** Think of someone in the class. Describe him or her to your group. The group guesses who it is.
12 Your group is going to a restaurant but you're too busy. Tell the group all the things you need to do around the house.	**11** You're going shopping. You want to buy new clothes. What do you want?	**10** Tell the group what you did last weekend.
13 You're at an Italian restaurant. Order a meal. Choose someone in the group to be the waiter.	**14** What clothing styles do you like/dislike? Tell the group.	**15** Tell the group your plans for this weekend.
24 You need to talk about something with your teacher. Choose someone to be the teacher and make an appointment.	**23** Describe what you did last vacation.	**22** You are buying some clothes. Ask a clerk for help. Choose someone in the group to be the clerk.
25 You're going to meet some people you met on the Internet. They've never seen you. Describe yourself.	**26** Imagine last night was wonderful. What did you do?	**27** What are you going to do when you retire?

4

Call your dentist's office and make an appointment. Choose someone in the group to be the receptionist.

5

You're at a coffee shop. Order a snack. Choose someone in the group to take your order.

6

Think about the last dream you had. Tell the group about it.

9

You work for a pizza delivery business. You have a customer on the phone. Choose someone to be the customer and ask for his/her delivery details.

8

What jobs don't you like to do around your house?

7

What did you do for your last birthday?

16

Call your doctor's office and make an appointment. Choose someone in the group to be the receptionist.

17

What jobs do you enjoy doing around the house?

18

Think of three different ways to say this date:
8 days from now.

21

What kind of personality do you have? What kind of people do you like?

20

You work in a bank. Someone in your group is applying for a credit card. Ask for his/her address, job and salary details.

19

Think of a famous movie star. Don't say the name. Describe him or her. The group guesses.

28

You're going out to a good restaurant. What are you going to wear?

29

You've just won a million dollars. What are you going to do?

30

Play again. Go backwards this time.

CHALLENGE

Vocabulary Game

Step 1:
Work with a partner. Look through Units 1–9. Find at least two words in every unit that you want to remember. Write them in the box.

Step 2:
Think of how to explain each word. You don't have to write it. Just think.

Units	Words
1	
2	
3	
4	
5	
6	
7	
8	
9	

Step 3:
Join another pair. Explain your words. The other pair will try to guess. You get one point for each correct guess. Which pair wins?

Listen and repeat.

> I need a haircut.   I'm just getting a trim.
> I have to make a deposit.   I need to stop at an ATM.
> I'd like a vanilla shake.   I'd like a burger with fries.

CONVERSATIONS

Listen and practice.

A. **Dori:**   Hi guys! What are you doing here?
   Larry: Harry needs *a haircut.*
   Lori: Yeah, he looks pretty hairy.
   Harry: Very funny. Actually, I'm just getting *a trim.*
   Larry: So where are you guys headed now?
   Dori: The bank. I have to *deposit some money.*
   Lori: And I need to *find an ATM and make a withdrawal.*

B. **Joe:**   Are you hungry?
   Scott: I could eat a horse!
   Server: May I help you?
   Joe: I'd like *a double cheeseburger and some fries.*
   Server: Anything to drink?
   Joe: *A vanilla shake.*
   Server: And you?
   Scott: This is on one bill. I'd like *two cheeseburgers, an order of fries, some onion rings, and a large chocolate shake.*
   Joe: Wow! It's on your bill, right?

PRACTICE

Practice the conversations with a classmate. Use this vocabulary.

a cut   a burger with fries

a perm   some fish 'n chips, an apple pie, some onion rings, and a chocolate milkshake

get some traveler's checks

cash a check   a strawberry shake

LISTEN

You will hear eight sentences. Write the number of each sentence under the correct picture.

a.

_____

c.

_____1_____

b.

_____

d.

_____

LISTEN AND UNDERSTAND

Listen to the conversation between a husband and wife. Check (✔) the places the husband went to.

☐ fast food restaurant   ☐ bank   ☐ supermarket
☐ post office   ☐ cleaners   ☐ drug store

Listen again and check (✔) the things the husband did.

☐ made a deposit   ☐ picked up the cleaning   ☐ bought stamps
☐ got two burgers   ☐ cashed a few checks   ☐ sent a package

A. Getting a Haircut

You are a hairdresser. Student B needs a haircut. Ask Student B the questions below.

Student A: How would you like me to cut it?
Student B: _____.
Student A: What about your bangs?
Student B: _____.
Student A: How do you wear your part?
Student B: _____.

Look at the pictures. Which haircut does Student B want?

a. 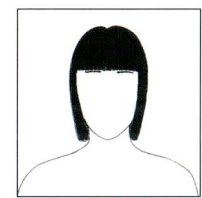   b. 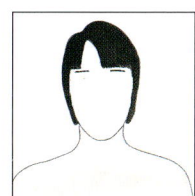   c.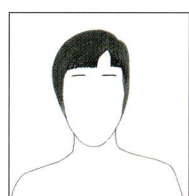

Now look at Student B's page. Practice the conversation again. This time you need a haircut.

B. Ordering from a Fast Food Menu

Work with a different classmate. Practice ordering from this fast food menu.

Sandwiches		Drinks	
Hamburger	$1.79	Pepsi, 7-Up, Diet Pepsi	
Cheeseburger	$1.99	*Small*	$1.09
Double cheeseburger	$2.69	*Medium*	$1.39
Chicken sandwich	$2.49	*Large*	$1.59
Fish sandwich	$2.69		
		Shakes (Vanilla, Strawberry, Chocolate)	
Sides		*Small*	$1.50
French fries	$1.09	*Medium*	$2.00
Onion rings	$1.09	*Large*	$2.75

A: May I help you?

B: Yes, I'll have a _____ .

A: Would you like anything else?

B: Yes, I'd like _____ .

or

That'll be all, thanks.

63

PAIRWORK
STUDENT B

A. Getting a Haircut

You need a haircut. Choose a style from the pictures below.

a. 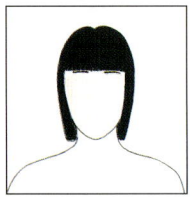 b. 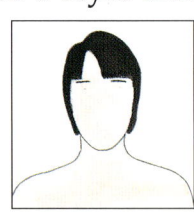 c.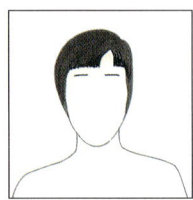

Student A is a hairdresser. Answer Student A's questions from the choices below.

Student A: _____?

Student B: About three inches off.
I'd like just a trim.
I want it very short.

Student A: _____?

Student B: Just a little off, please.
They're OK.
Could you cut them above my eyebrows, please?

Student A: _____?

Student B: Part it in the middle.
Part it on the left side.
Part it more on the right.

Now look at Student A's page. Practice the conversation again. This time you are the hairdresser.

B. Ordering from a Fast Food Menu

Work with a different classmate. Practice ordering from this fast food menu.

Sandwiches		Drinks	
Hamburger	$1.79	Pepsi, 7-Up, Diet Pepsi	
Cheeseburger	$1.99	Small	$1.09
Double cheeseburger	$2.69	Medium	$1.39
Chicken sandwich	$2.49	Large	$1.59
Fish sandwich	$2.69		
		Shakes (Vanilla, Strawberry, Chocolate)	
Sides		Small	$1.50
French fries	$1.09	Medium	$2.00
Onion rings	$1.09	Large	$2.75

A: May I help you?

B: Yes, I'll have a _____ .

A: Would you like anything else?

B: Yes, I'd like _____ .

or

That'll be all, thanks.

PRONUNCIATION

A. In English, one word in each sentence gets the most stress. If you don't stress that word, people can't understand your English very well. This word is the most important word in the sentence.

Listen to these examples:

> I'd like a cheeseburger and **fries**.
>
> I need to make a de**posit**.
>
> How much is a **book** of stamps?

B. Listen to the sentences and underline the word that is stressed the most.

1. I'd like to make a withdrawal.

2. I'd like a perm.

3. I need to cash this.

4. This time I only want a trim, please.

5. I'd like a chocolate shake.

C. Practice this conversation with a classmate several times. Each time, choose a different food to order. Think about which words to stress.

A: May I help you?
B: Yes, I'd like to order a hamburger
                            some fries
                            a milkshake
                            a cola
                            some onion rings
A: Would you like anything else?
B: No, that'll be all, thanks.

CHALLENGE

A. Work with a classmate. Write down the place for the activities below and think of a phrase for each one.

Activity	Place	Phrase
Take money out of your account	*bank*	*I'd like to make a withdrawal.*
Look at the food on the menu	_____	_____
Send a letter faster than usual	_____	_____
Receive money from a check	_____	_____
Book a table	_____	_____
Start a new bank account	_____	_____
Buy stamps	_____	_____
Pay for your meal	_____	_____

B. Work with a classmate. Imagine you are the people in one of the pictures. Have a short conversation. Continue with the other pictures.

1.

3.

2.

4.

Listen and repeat.

What should I pick up for dinner?
What did you buy?
I'm on a new diet.

How about some steaks?
Soft drinks and corn chips.
What's it called?

CONVERSATIONS

Listen and practice.

A. **June:** What should I pick up for *dinner*?
Pat: How about some *big, juicy steaks*?
June: You're not serious, are you? Red meat isn't healthy.
Pat: I'm so tired of *tofu*. Why did I decide to live with a vegetarian?
June: I'm not vegetarian! I eat *fish and chicken* sometimes.
Pat: And lots of *seaweed*.
June: Quit complaining! If you don't like my choices, you can always do the shopping yourself!

B. **Steve:** What did you buy?
Kim: *Soft drinks, potato chips, candy, and popcorn.*
Steve: I mean, what did you get for *dinner*?
Kim: That is *dinner*!
Steve: Are you crazy?
Kim: I'm on a new diet. It's called the *junk food* diet.
Steve: What???
Kim: Just kidding. They're snacks for the baseball game.

PRACTICE

Practice the conversations with a classmate. Use this vocabulary.

salad	tacos	bananas	lamb
lunch	hamburgers	milkshakes	rice
eggs	beans	tuna	potatoes
chocolate	vegetables	ice cream	fat
pork chops	pasta	yogurt	junk food

LISTEN

Listen. Match the numbers of the conversations to the pictures.

LISTEN AND UNDERSTAND

Listen to the conversations between two roommates. Match the words in the box to the different items.

1.
| loaf | bar | tube | box | jar |

_____ of toothpaste
_____ of laundry detergent
_____ of soap
_____ of mayonnaise
_____ of bread

2.
| bag | box | carton |

_____ of cereal
_____ of milk
_____ of vanilla ice cream
_____ of potato chips

You are making a shopping list. Your roommate (Student B) is looking in the refrigerator. Ask Student B about the items on the shopping list below. Check (✔) the foods you need to buy.

Here are the questions you can ask:

Is there any _____ ?

Are there any _____ ?

eggs
ketchup
pears
chicken
tofu
lettuce
tomatoes
yogurt

Now Student B is making a shopping list. Look in the refrigerator and answer Student B's questions.

Here are the answers you can give:

Yes, there is some _____ .   No, there isn't any _____ .

Yes, there are some _____ .   No, there aren't any _____ .

69

PAIRWORK
STUDENT B

Your roommate (Student A) is making a shopping list. Look in the refrigerator and answer Student A's questions.

Here are the answers you can give:

Yes, there is some _____ .

Yes, there are some _____ .

No, there isn't any _____ .

No, there aren't any _____ .

Now you are making a shopping list. Student A is looking in the refrigerator. Ask Student A about the items on the shopping list below. Check (✔) the foods you need to buy.

Here are the questions you can ask:

Is there any _____ ?

Are there any _____ ?

ground beef
orange juice
bananas
carrots
mayonnaise
fish
cheese
soft drinks

PRONUNCIATION

A. As you know, English spelling and English pronunciation can be very different. Here are some words. Next to them is an easy spelling to help you pronounce them. Listen and repeat.

1. aisle   *I'll*
2. mayonnaise *may-naize*
3. salmon   *sa-mon*
4. aspirin   *a-sprin*
5. carton   *car'n*

B. Sometimes in English, a syllable is dropped from a word. Listen to these words. Cross out the missing syllable.

1. fam~~i~~ly
2. broccoli
3. bakery
4. chocolate
5. beverage
6. vegetables

C. Look at the pictures. Complete these dialogues with a classmate. Use the words in the box.

carton	salmon	vegetable	mayonnaise	broccoli	aisle

1. **A:** Where is the _____ ?
   B: It's down _____ 8.

2. **A:** Did you get a _____ of milk?
   B: Sorry, I forgot. But here's some chocolate cake from the bakery.

3. **A:** How about tuna sandwiches for lunch?
   B: We're out of _____ .

4. **A:** How about _____ for dinner?
   B: Not again! Any other _____ but broccoli!

Listen and check your answers.

71

CHALLENGE

Food Bingo

How many foods do you know? Walk around the room. Ask your classmates questions about the foods on the chart. If the person says "yes," write his or her name in the square. When you have five in a row, shout Bingo!

Here are some questions you can ask:

Did you eat _____ this week?

Do you like _____ ?

Did you buy _____ this week?

Listen and repeat.

So what brings you here today?
Are you feeling okay?
It looks like you have a cavity.

I've had indigestion since last night.
No, I have a bad headache.
Do I need a filling?

CONVERSATIONS

Listen and practice.

A. **Dr. Robinson:** I hear you have a toothache.
   Kari: Yeah. My tooth began hurting yesterday morning.
   Dr. Robinson: Let me take a look. Yep, it looks like you have a cavity.
   Kari: Do I need a filling?
   Dr. Robinson: Yes, but you can watch a video while I do it.

B. **Dr. Jones:** So what brings you here today?
   Barbara: I've had *a bad cough* for a week.
   Dr. Jones: Have you had *a fever*?
   Barbara: I don't think so.
   Dr. Jones: Did you have *the flu* first?
   Barbara: No, it began with *a cold* but that was three weeks ago.
   Dr. Jones: Let me take a look.

Note: There are two ways to talk about pain.

	knee			*headache*
1. My	*tooth* hurts.	2.	I have a	*toothache*.
	leg			*stomachache*
	back			*backache*

PRACTICE

Here are some health problems. Circle the ones you think are serious enough for a visit to the doctor.

a headache	the chills	a stomachache
dizziness	a cough	a backache
a sore throat	insomnia (can't sleep)	a virus
allergies	nausea/vomiting/throwing up	a fever
indigestion	a toothache	skin rash

Practice conversation B with a classmate. Use this vocabulary.

LISTEN

Listen. Match the numbers of the conversations to the pictures.

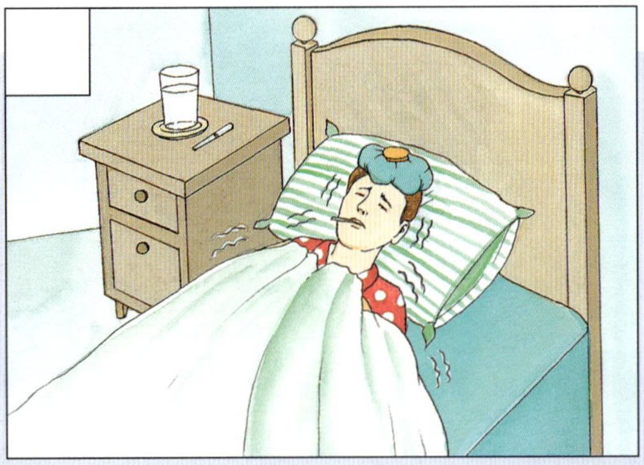

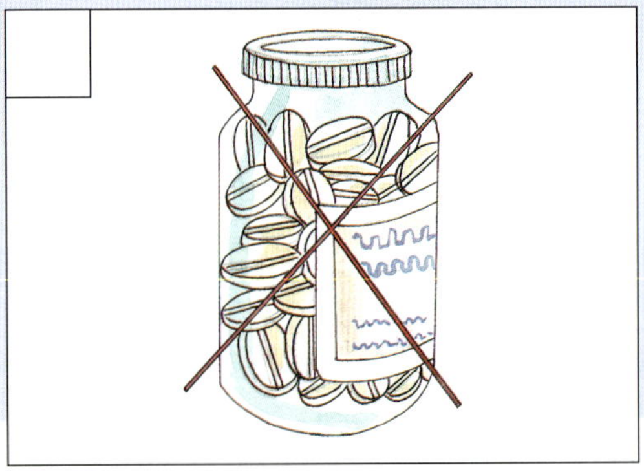

LISTEN AND UNDERSTAND

Listen to the conversation between a doctor and patient. Circle the correct answers.

1. The patient has a headache.   yes   no
2. The patient has a sore throat.   yes   no
3. The patient has children in day care.   yes   no
4. The doctor checked the patient's whole body.   yes   no
5. The doctor knows the problem.   yes   no

Work with Student B. How many medical problems do you know in English? Write them below.

1. <u>sore throat</u>
2. _____
3. _____
4. _____
5. _____

6. _____
7. _____
8. _____
9. _____
10. _____

You and Student B are co-workers. You aren't feeling well today. Practice the conversation.

Student A: I'm not feeling too good today.

Student B: _____

Student A: I have a sore throat.
or
I feel really tired.

Student B: _____

Student A: I'm making a lot of mistakes.
or
I also have a bad cold.

Student B: _____

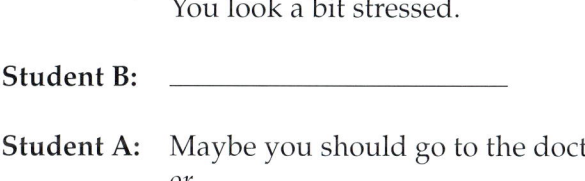

Now Student B isn't feeling well. Practice the conversation.

Student A: Are you feeling okay?

Student B: _____

Student A: I heard the 'flu's going around.
or
You look a bit stressed.

Student B: _____

Student A: Maybe you should go to the doctor.
or
Get some exercise. That will help.

Student B: _____

Turn to Student B's page. Practice the conversations again.

PAIRWORK
STUDENT B

Work with Student A. How many medical problems do you know in English? Write them below.

1. *sore throat*
2. _____
3. _____
4. _____
5. _____

6. _____
7. _____
8. _____
9. _____
10. _____

You and Student A are co-workers. Student A isn't feeling well today. Practice the conversation.

Student A: _____

Student B: What's the problem?

Student A: _____

Student B: You're working too hard.
or
Sounds like the 'flu.

Student A: _____

Student B: You should drink lots of orange juice.
or
You need a break. Take some time off.

Now you aren't feeling well. Practice the conversation.

Student A: _____

Student B: No, I have a bad headache.
or
No, I feel a little weak.

Student A: _____

Student B: I also have a light fever.
or
That would explain my bad temper.

Student A: _____

Student B: Yeah. I think I'll do that.

Turn to Student A's page. Practice the conversations again.

PRONUNCIATION

A. In spoken English, words are connected. This is called linking. Listen to the following sentences:

> I have a headache.
>
> I need an aspirin.
>
> My fever is high.

Words that begin with vowels (*a, e, i, o, u*) are linked to the word before.

B. Listen to these sentences. Connect the words that are linked.

1. I have terrible allergies.

2. I had insomnia all week.

3. My body aches and I have a runny nose.

4. That's awful.

5. Is it serious?

6. I'll take a blood sample.

C. Connect the words that are linked. Practice these conversations with a classmate.

1. **A:** What's the problem?

   B: I have a bad sore throat.

   A: Do you have any other symptoms?

   B: I also have a fever of 100.

2. **A:** How long have you been ill?

   B: For about a week.

   A: Why didn't you come in sooner?

   B: I didn't think it was serious.

CHALLENGE

A. **What do you do when you're sick? Write your answers to the questions. Then ask a classmate the questions and write his or her answers.**

What do you do when you …	You	Classmate
1. have a headache?		
2. have a cold?		
3. have the flu?		
4. have a stomachache?		
5. have a backache?		
6. feel stressed?		
7. have indigestion?		
8. have insomnia?		
9. _____? (add your own idea)		

Compare your answers. How many are the same? How many are different? Discuss the answers that are different. Finally, share your answers with another pair.

B. **Work in small groups. Answer the questions below.**

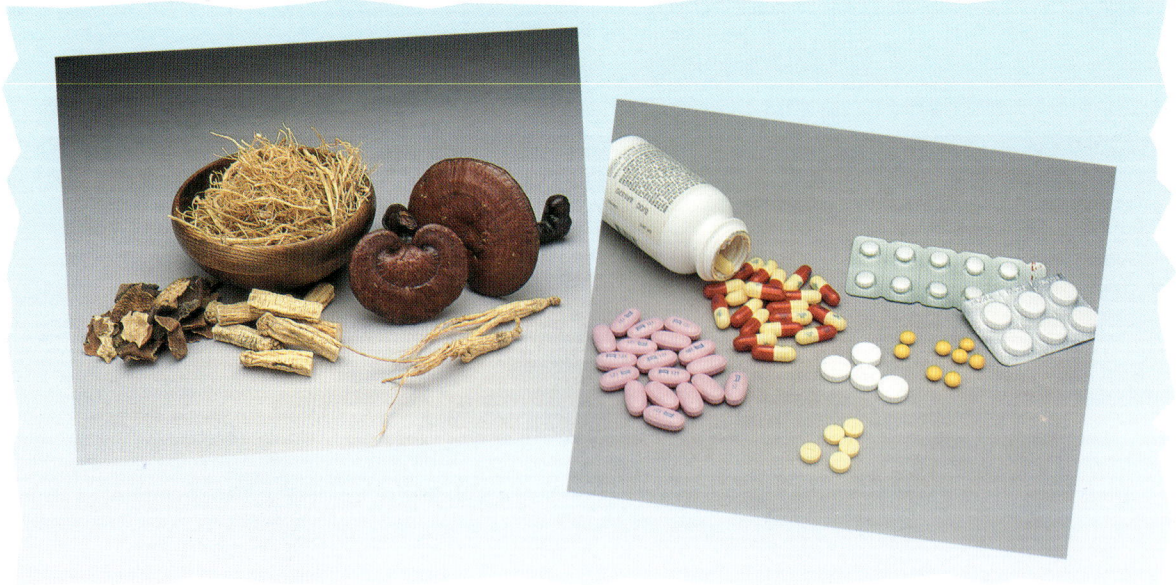

1. What is the difference between traditional Chinese medicine and western medicine?
2. For what health problems would you use traditional Chinese medicine? Western medicine?

Listen and repeat.

What kind of music do you like?	I like jazz.
Do you like rap music?	No, I don't like it at all.
I love rock music.	I prefer reggae.

CONVERSATION

Listen and practice.

Kelly:	My husband and I are completely opposite.
Ginger:	How so?
Kelly:	I really like to go out and meet people. He loves to stay home and read.
Ginger:	That's not unusual. Is there anything else?
Kelly:	I prefer rock and roll. Guess what he likes?
Ginger:	Classical?
Kelly:	You're right. There are other things, too. I like having lots of pets around.
Ginger:	And I bet your husband doesn't like them.
Kelly:	He doesn't care for them at all. They make him sneeze.
Ginger:	Do you have any similar interests?
Kelly:	I can't think of one.
Ginger:	Why did you get married then?
Kelly:	We loved each other!
Ginger:	At least you agreed on the important one!

PRACTICE

Choose one kind of music you really like; one you don't like; and something in the middle. Talk to a classmate about your taste in music. Use the words in the box or any other words you know that describe types of music.

Classical	JAZZ	Reggae	Salsa
Hip Hop			SWING
Rap	Folk	Country	Bluegrass
the Blues	Rock	HEAVY METAL	Samba

I love _____ .	I don't mind _____ .	I don't care for_____ .
I really like _____ .	I dislike _____ .	I hate _____ .
I like _____ .	I'm not really excited about	I can't stand _____ .
_____ is OK.	_____ .	I'm crazy about _____ .

LISTEN

Listen to the conversations. Decide if the speaker loves something, thinks it's OK, or hates it. Put a check (✔) in the correct box.

likes/loves it	thinks it's OK/doesn't mind it	dislikes/hates it
1. ✔		
2.		
3.		
4.		
5.		

LISTEN AND UNDERSTAND

You will hear a conversation about movies. What does the woman think about the movies below? Draw lines to match the movies on the left with the phrases on the right.

1. violent movies
2. action movies
3. romance movies
4. comedies
5. Tom Hanks movies
6. foreign movies

thinks they're OK

loves them

really likes them

doesn't mind them

doesn't care for them

hates them

Five of your co-workers, Gina, George, Mina, Robin, and Alex, have their birthdays this month. You and Student B are planning an office party for them. Here are the foods you are thinking of buying:

| pizza | steak | salmon | stir fry vegetables | chicken |

Work with Student B. Ask questions to complete the chart and answer Student B's questions.

Example: What about pizza?
Yes. Gina loves pizza.

Here are more sentences you can use:

She/he loves _____ .

She/he really likes _____ .

She/he likes _____ .

She/he dislikes _____ .

She/he doesn't care for _____ .

She/he hates _____ .

She/he can't stand _____ .

She/he doesn't mind _____ .

She/he thinks _____ is OK.

Names	likes/loves it	thinks it's OK/ doesn't mind it	dislikes/hates it
Gina	pizza		
George		salmon	
Mina	salmon		steak
Robin	chicken		stir fry vegetables
Alex		pizza	

What food can they all agree on?

PAIRWORK
STUDENT B

Five of your co-workers, Gina, George, Mina, Robin, and Alex, have their birthdays this month. You and Student A are planning an office party for them. Here are the foods you are thinking of buying:

| pizza | steak | salmon | stir fry vegetables | chicken |

Work with Student A. Ask questions to complete the chart and answer Student A's questions.

Example: What about pizza?
No. George hates pizza.

Here are more sentences you can use:

She/he loves _____ .

She/he really likes _____ .

She/he likes _____ .

She/he dislikes _____ .

She/he doesn't care for _____ .

She/he hates _____ .

She/he can't stand _____ .

She/he doesn't mind _____ .

She/he thinks _____ is OK.

Names	likes/loves it	thinks it's OK/ doesn't mind it	dislikes/hates it
Gina		steak	salmon
George	steak		pizza
Mina		stir fry vegetables	
Robin		steak	
Alex	stir fry vegetables		salmon

What food can they all agree on?

PRONUNCIATION

A. Many small words in English are unstressed or reduced. Here are some common ones:

and	→	'n
to	→	ta
of	→	a
or	→	'r
you	→	ya

Listen to these examples:

rock and roll	*rock'n roll*
love to dance	*love ta dance*
lots of music	*lotsa music*
classical or jazz	*classical 'r jazz*
You like it?	*Ya like it?*

B. Fill in the blanks with the word you hear.

A: Let's go out _____ dance.

B: _____ know, I hate _____ dance.

A: Then let's listen _____ some music. We've got _____ choices.

B: I prefer jazz _____ the blues.

A: My favorites are jazz _____ the blues, so let's listen _____ both.

C. Practice the chant.

I love to sing

I love to dance

Put on some music

And give me a chance.

You don't want to join me?

Well, just sit and listen,

I'm going to rock

And you'll see what you're missing.

CHALLENGE

Bingo

Walk around the room. Find a person to match the sentences and write his or her name in the square. When you have five in a row, shout Bingo!

		Answer
Examples:	Do you dislike going to the dentist?	Yes.
	Do you care for fast food?	No.

loves watching basketball	thinks English is OK	dislikes going to the dentist	gets excited about computers	loves rap music
_____	_____	_____	_____	_____
really likes snakes	gets excited about flying in an airplane	loves shopping	doesn't care for fast food	doesn't mind doing the dishes
_____	_____	_____	_____	_____
doesn't mind math	thinks classical music is OK	doesn't care for strawberries	really likes using the Internet	can't stand getting up early
_____	_____	_____	_____	_____
hates TV commercials	likes speaking English	really likes watching sports on TV	loves talking on the phone	doesn't mind cleaning house
_____	_____	_____	_____	_____
can't stand violent movies	thinks homework is not bad	is not excited about going dancing	loves jazz	doesn't care for video games
_____	_____	_____	_____	_____

Listen and repeat.

You look a little down.   I'm feeling a bit depressed.
How are you feeling?   I'm really excited.
Are you OK?   I'm a little tired.

CONVERSATION

Listen and practice.

Sara: You look a little down. Are you OK?

Kenji: I'm not sure. I'm always really tired, but I sleep a lot.

Sara: How long has this been going on?

Kenji: About a month. I'm feeling a bit depressed, too.

Sara: How long have you been here?

Kenji: About six months.

Sara: Are you doing fun things with friends?

Kenji: No, I don't feel like going out.

Sara: You know, you might have culture shock.

Kenji: What's that?

Sara: When you live in another culture, it can be a big shock to your system. People get different symptoms. Some people sleep, some people have insomnia. Some people eat a lot, some people don't eat enough.

Kenji: How do you know so much about it?

Sara: I got it when I moved to Hong Kong. But it went away after a few months.

PRACTICE

Check (✔) all the words that describe yourself right now.

☐ happy   ☐ excited   ☐ relaxed   ☐ energetic
☐ interested   ☐ bored   ☐ nervous   ☐ stressed
☐ depressed   ☐ worried   ☐ tense   ☐ exhausted

Tell a classmate how you are feeling.

LISTEN

Listen. Match the numbers of the conversations to the pictures.

LISTEN AND UNDERSTAND

Listen to the conversations. After each one, choose two or three words from the list to finish each sentence.

happy	relaxed	energetic	depressed
nervous	exhausted	excited	tense
tired	bored	sad	worried

1. David is probably feeling _____ .

2. Jim is probably feeling _____ .

3. Maria is probably feeling _____ .

PAIRWORK
STUDENT A

Find out how the people in the chart are feeling. Ask Student B questions and match the words in the box to the names in the chart. Find out why the people are feeling that way.

down	depressed	energetic	nervous	tired

Example:

A: Who is depressed?   *or*   A: How is Kim feeling?
B: Kim is.   B: Depressed.
A: Why does she feel depressed?   A: Why?
B: She got 40% on a test.   B: She got 40% on a test.

	Kim	Sam	Masako	Sue	Jack
Feeling	depressed				
Reason	got 40% on a test				

Now answer Student B's questions about the people in the chart below.

	Luke	Kieran	Jane	Kheng	Steve
Feeling	frustrated	sad	worried	relaxed	exhausted
Reason					

PAIRWORK
STUDENT B

Answer Student A's questions about the people in the chart.

Example:

A: Who is depressed?   *or:*   A: How is Kim feeling?
B: Kim is.   B: Depressed.
A: Why does she feel depressed?   A: Why?
B: She got 40% on a test.   B: She got 40% on a test.

	Kim	Sam	Masako	Sue	Jack
Feeling	depressed	tired	energetic	nervous	down
Reason	40%				*Dear Mr Walsh We regret to tell you that we have given the designer job to another applicant. Thank you for your interest in our company.*

Now find out how the people in the chart below are feeling. Ask Student A questions and match the words in the box to the names in the chart. Find out why the people are feeling that way.

> exhausted   frustrated   relaxed   sad   worried

	Luke	Kieran	Jane	Kheng	Steve
Feeling	*frustrated*				
Reason	*his car broke down*				

PRONUNCIATION

A. It is important in English to pronounce the final sounds. You don't want to drop them. Listen to these words and then say them. Pay special attention to the final sounds.

nervou**s**	exci**ted**	energe**tic**	sa**d**	ten**se**

B. If it is difficult to pronounce the final sound, try linking the word by adding a phrase like *every day* or *all the time*. Then the final sound becomes a beginning sound. Linking helps make the final sound more clear.

Listen and practice saying these sentences.

1. I feel excited every day.

2. I feel nervous all the time.

3. I feel sad every day.

4. I feel energetic all the time.

C. Work with a classmate. Follow the example and make dialogues for 1–4 below.

Example:

A: How does he feel?
B: He feels *tired*.
A: Is he always *tired*?
B: He feels *tired all the time*.

1. How does he feel?

2. How does she feel?

3. How does the dog feel?

4. How do you feel?

Ask your classmate.

CHALLENGE

A. **Jimmy, Jerry, Jenny, Jeffrey, Joanie, Jackie, and Johnny all live in the same dormitory. One of them is very lucky. He or she has never been depressed or down in his or her life! Can you guess who it is? Read the clues. Work in small groups to decide.**

Clues

1. Jerry gets really worried when he has a test to prepare for.
2. Johnny always looks relaxed, even when he gets bad news.
3. People think Jimmy and Jenny are brother and sister because they always feel the same way.
4. Johnny and Joanie get along very well.
5. Jeffrey is a happy guy. He likes everyone equally. He doesn't have a best friend.
6. Joanie loves to go out with her friends and listen to their problems. She wants to be a psychologist.
7. Jenny never cries when she feels down.
8. Jimmy enjoys meeting people and finding out about their lives. If they have problems, he likes to help them.
9. Jackie and Joanie are best friends with the person who is never depressed.

B. **Work in small groups. Look at the words below. When was the last time you felt that way? What made you feel that way? Tell your group.**

angry

embarrassed

excited

disappointed

Listen and repeat.

Where do you want to go for vacation?	How about camping?
Staying in a hotel is easier.	Yes, but camping is much better.
Shall we rent a cabin?	Sleeping under the stars will be more romantic.

CONVERSATION

Listen and practice.

Allan: Where do you want to go for vacation?

Linda: How about camping?

Allan: Camping? That's so much work. Staying in a hotel is a lot easier.

Linda: Allan, what do you mean? Camping is so much better. The scenery is more beautiful, the air is cleaner, you get more exercise, it's healthier for you, and the food tastes fresher.

Allan: Yeah, and first you have to hike a day to get to the campsite.

Linda: We can choose something we can drive to.

Allan: Then it will be too crowded.

Linda: I've got an idea. Let's go to the ocean.

Allan: Well, since it's September, it will be less crowded. Shall we rent a cabin?

Linda: No, silly, we'll get a camping spot near the beach. Sleeping under the stars will be much more romantic than staying in a cabin!

Allan: Hmm. At least it will be cheaper.

PRACTICE

Work with a classmate. The two of you are planning your next vacation. You are deciding between a cruise to Alaska and helicopter skiing in the Canadian Rockies. Use the words below to compare the two options.

cheap	beautiful
expensive	romantic
fun	safe
interesting	enjoyable
boring	difficult

Example: **A:** The cruise is easier.

B: Helicopter skiing is more exciting.

LISTEN

Listen to the conversations. Write the letter of the correct picture next to the comparison words.

1. a.   b.

_____ more expensive

3. a.   b.

_____ older

2. a.   b.

_____ faster

4. a.   b.

_____ easier

LISTEN AND UNDERSTAND

Listen to the conversation. Check (✔) which information is true.

☐ friendlier people   ☐ friendlier people
☐ cleaner air   ☐ cleaner air
☐ safer feeling   ☐ safer feeling
☐ variety of food   ☐ variety of food
☐ more convenient   ☐ more convenient
☐ more driving   ☐ more driving
☐ higher prices   ☐ higher prices
☐ more to do   ☐ more to do
☐ more relaxing   ☐ more relaxing

You and Student B both have a picture of a park. Ask and answer questions to find what is different using the words in the box. Write the differences below.

boy/girl (heavy/thin)
dog on the left/right (big/small)
man/woman on the bench (old/young)
car in front/behind (fast/slow)

green/blue bench (long/short)
hotdogs/fries (cheap, expensive)
businessman/businesswoman (tall/short)

Example:

Student A: Who's heavier, the girl or the boy?
Student B: The girl is heavier.
Student A: In my picture, the boy is heavier than the girl.

DIFFERENCES

In my picture:

1. _the boy is heavier than the girl._
2. _____
3. _____
4. _____
5. _____
6. _____
7. _____
8. _____
9. _____
10. _____

PAIRWORK
STUDENT B

You and Student A both have a picture of a park. Ask and answer questions to find what is different using the words in the box. Write the differences below.

boy/girl (heavy/thin)	green/blue bench (long/short)
dog on the left/right (big/small)	hotdogs/fries (cheap, expensive)
man/woman on the bench (old/young)	businessman/businesswoman (tall/short)
car in front/behind (fast/slow)	

Example:

Student A: Who's heavier, the girl or the boy?
Student B: The girl is heavier.
Student A: In my picture, the boy is heavier than the girl.

DIFFERENCES

In my picture:

1. *the girl is heavier than the boy.*
2. _____
3. _____
4. _____
5. _____
6. _____
7. _____
8. _____
9. _____
10. _____

PRONUNCIATION

A. The *er* sound can be difficult to pronounce. Listen to these words. Then, say them slowly so that you have time to make the *er* sound.

taller	shorter
older	faster
easier	younger

B. Listen to these sentences. Circle the adjective you hear.

1. tall   taller
2. spicy   spicier
3. healthy   healthier
4. big   bigger
5. rainy   rainier
6. old   older

C. With a partner, make sentences comparing the pictures. Here are some words you can use.

big	strong	fast	short	smart
small	weak	slow	long	dumb

Example: A is smaller than B.

1.

A   B

2.

A   B

3.

A   B

4.   5.

A   B   A   B

95

CHALLENGE

A. Walk around the room and ask other students the questions below. Answer in complete sentences.

Which do you like better?

1. Big cars or fast cars?
2. Studying English or studying another subject? Which one?
3. Being with a lot of people or being with a few people? Why?
4. Using a computer or writing by hand? Why?
5. Hot weather or cold weather? Why?
6. Working indoors or working outdoors? Why?
7. Listening to rock music or listening to jazz?
8. Getting presents or giving presents? Why?
9. Cooking or cleaning?
10. The morning or the evening? Why?

Share some of your answers with the class.

B. Your school has to move to a different part of town. There are two possible locations. Ask your teacher where they are.

Location 1: _____   Location 2: _____

Divide into two groups. Each group chooses one of the locations. Think of five reasons why that location is a better choice.

1. _____
2. _____
3. _____
4. _____
5. _____

Now give your reasons to the other group and listen to their reasons. Take a vote on which location will be best.

Listen and repeat.

I'd like to get a new job.
I can do a little word processing.
My kids can use the Internet better than me.

Are you good with computers?
Can you use the Internet?
I think you need some training.

CONVERSATIONS

Listen and practice.

A. Sue: Have you ever worked as a tour guide before?
   Pam: When I was in college, I worked for a travel agency.
   Sue: What skills do you have to be a tour guide?
   Pam: I love traveling, and I can memorize information about a place quickly. Also, I'm energetic and I can speak several languages.

B. Martha: I'm really tired of my office job. I'd like to get something more interesting with higher pay.
   Harry: Computer jobs pay very well.
   Martha: I can do a little word processing, but that's about it. I barely know what e-mail is!
   Harry: Can you use the Internet?
   Martha: My kids can use the Internet better than me.
   Harry: I think you need to get some training.
   Martha: I agree. But who can find the time?

PRACTICE

What skills do you need for the jobs below? Match the jobs with the skills in the box.

child care worker	fast-food clerk	waiter/waitress	bank clerk
_____	_____	_____	_____
_____	_____	_____	_____
_____	_____	_____	_____
_____	_____	_____	_____

outgoing   organized (have a plan)   energetic   patient   good with people
friendly   good with numbers   fast worker   honest   creative (have new ideas)

Practice this short conversation with a classmate. Use the vocabulary above.

A: What skills do you have to be a _____ ?
B: I'm _____ .

LISTEN

Listen. Match the numbers of the conversations to the jobs.

☐ tour guide   ☐ auto mechanic

☐ sales person   ☐ delivery person

☐ hotel staff   ☐ computer programmer

LISTEN AND UNDERSTAND

Listen to the job interview. Check (✔) the experience and skills the woman has.

☐ manager   ☐ good with people

☐ secretary   ☐ college degree

☐ spreadsheets   ☐ math

☐ word processing   ☐ teacher

☐ computer programming   ☐ sales

You are the editor of a big newspaper. You are looking for a reporter to cover stories in Europe. You placed the advertisement below in your newspaper.

The Daily Planet

We are looking for a reporter to cover international news around Europe. The successful applicant will need to:

- travel to where the stories are
- sometimes work in war zones
- do lots of interviews
- finish the stories in good time
- send us the stories over the Internet
- work irregular hours
- take photographs

Does this sound like you? Send your resume to hubert_brown@dailyplanet.com

Work with a classmate. Student B is going to interview for the job. Write interview questions to ask Student B to see if he or she has the skills for the job.

Use these phrases:

Do you know how to …?	*Can you speak other languages?*
Are you good at …?	
Do you like to …?	
Can you …?	

Now interview Student B. Is he or she the right person for the job?

You are looking for a job. You see this job advertisement in a newspaper. It is a job you are interested in.

The Daily Planet

We are looking for a reporter to cover international news around Europe. The successful applicant will need to:

- travel to where the stories are
- sometimes work in war zones
- do lots of interviews
- finish the stories in good time
- send us the stories over the Internet
- work irregular hours
- take photographs

Does this sound like you? Send your resume to hubert_brown@dailyplanet.com

Work with a classmate. You have an interview with Student A. Write a list of the job skills you have that Student A will want to know about.

Use these phrases:

I know how to …   *I'm good at working fast.*

I'm good at … _____

I like to … _____

I can … _____

_____

_____

Now go for an interview with Student A. Good luck!

PRONUNCIATION

A. The pronunciation of *can* and *can't* is different from the spelling. In a sentence, *can* is pronounced *kn*. It has no stress. The other verb gets stressed. *Can't* is stressed but the *t* is not really pronounced. Listen to these examples:

> I *kn* **type**. (I can type.)   I *kn* **fix cars**. (I can fix cars.)
>
> I *kan'* **type**. (I can't type.)   I *kan'* **fix** cars. (I can't fix cars.)

If you say *can* strongly, people will think you are saying the negative *can't*.

B. Listen to six sentences. Circle the word you hear each time.

1. (can)   can't   4. can   can't

2. can   can't   5. can   can't

3. can   can't   6. can   can't

C. Listen and repeat.

1. I can do word processing.

2. I can't use a database.

3. I can type 60 words per minute.

4. I can't do math in my head.

5. I can speak two languages fluently.

D. With a classmate, discuss things you can and can't do. The listener should say *positive* (+) or *negative* (–) to check whether or not he or she understood.

Examples:

A: I can play the piano.
B: Positive.
A: That's right.

A: I can speak French.
B: Negative.
A: No, I was trying to be positive.

Each partner should say at least five sentences.

CHALLENGE

Journeys Talent Show!

A. **You are organizing a class talent show. You need to find people for the acts on the program. Ask your classmates questions to find out what they can do. Complete the program with their names and details of their act. (Note: try to find a different classmate for each act.)**

Examples: **A:** Do you know how to dance? **A:** Can you do magic tricks?
           B: Yes, I do. **B:** Yes, I can.
           A: Can you do the tango? **A:** What kind of tricks can you do?

Talent Show Program

Act		Name	Details
1. Dance			
2. Music			
3. Singing			
4. Comedy (make people laugh)			
5. Magic			

Tell the class about the acts on your program.

B. **Look at the jobs. Put checks (✔) next to the ones that interest you.**

☐ factory worker   ☐ farmer   ☐ airline pilot   ☐ psychologist

☐ architect   ☐ sales person   ☐ teacher   ☐ engineer

☐ child care worker   ☐ bank clerk   ☐ translator   ☐ computer programmer

☐ nurse   ☐ mechanic   ☐ waiter   ☐ tour guide

☐ photographer   ☐ secretary   ☐ politician   ☐ musician

Work in small groups. Tell your group about two jobs that you would be good at. Tell your group about two jobs that you are not interested in.

Listen and repeat.

I'm dying for a milkshake.
What do we need?
Now what?
Done.

I know how to make them.
First, fill your blender with ice cream.
Pour in a cup of milk.
Now add some chocolate sauce and turn it on.

CONVERSATIONS

Listen and practice.

A. **Gary:** I'm dying for a *chocolate* milkshake.
Karen: We can make them here. I know how to do it.
Gary: Great. What do we need?
Karen: First get your blender and fill it with *vanilla ice cream*.
Gary: Now what?
Karen: Pour in a cup of milk. Add some *chocolate sauce*.
Gary: Done.
Karen: Now turn it on. Keep going until it's creamy. If it's too thick, add a little more milk.
Gary: Mmm. This tastes great!

B. **Donna:** Let's have some popcorn while we watch the video.
Roger: I don't know how to make popcorn.
Donna: You're kidding! It's so easy.
Roger: Well, show me.
Donna: Put some oil in a pan and heat it.
Roger: OK.
Donna: Put in a small cup of popcorn.
Roger: And just let it cook?
Donna: No, keep shaking the pan so it doesn't burn. When the popcorn stops popping, it's done.

PRACTICE

Practice Conversation A with a classmate. Use these words.

strawberry	strawberry ice cream	fresh strawberries
banana	vanilla ice cream	sliced bananas
mango	mango ice cream	sliced mangoes

103

LISTEN

L isten. **Match the numbers of the conversations to the pictures.**

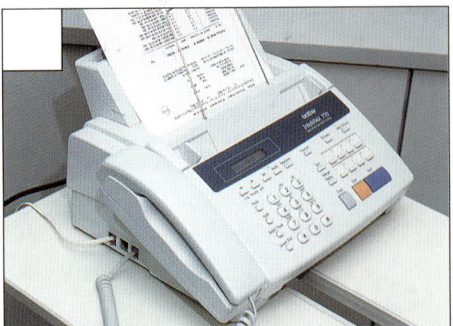

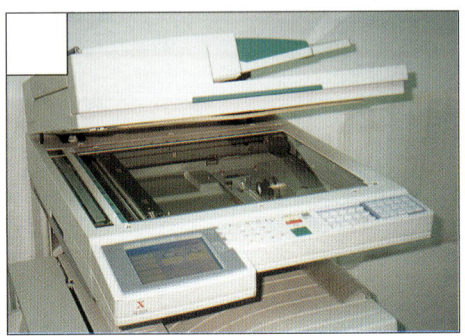

LISTEN AND UNDERSTAND

A. **Listen to the driving instructions. Number the sentences in the correct order.**

_____ Put the car in gear.

_____ Turn the key until the engine starts.

_____ Release the hand brake.

_____ Press down on the foot brake.

_____ Take your foot off the brake.

B. **Listen to the people talk about how to make French toast. Number the sentences in the correct order.**

_____ cook both sides

_____ dip the bread in the egg

_____ beat the eggs

_____ heat the pan

_____ add milk

_____ sprinkle with powdered sugar

You and Student B are going to take turns drawing pictures. Give instructions to Student B so that he or she can draw the pictures below.

Useful language

Start with a …	draw	a circle	in the middle
Then …	make	a line	next to the …
After that, …	put	a square	under the …
Finally, …	add	a triangle	at the top

1.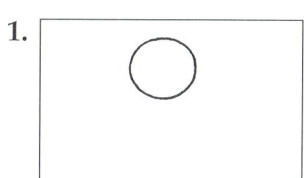
2.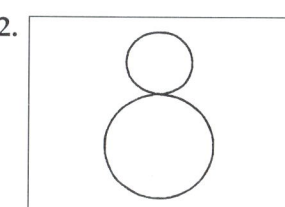
3.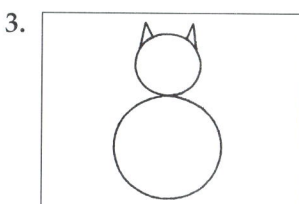
4.

5.
6.
7.

Now listen to Student B's instructions and draw the pictures.

1.
2.
3.
4.

5.
6.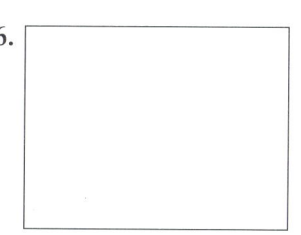
7.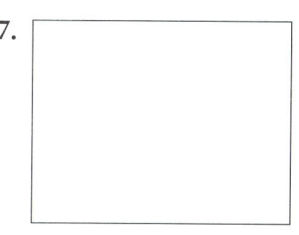

Show your pictures to Student B. Did you follow the instructions well? Look at Student B's pictures. How did he or she do? Share your pictures with the rest of the class.

PAIRWORK
STUDENT B

You and Student A are going to take turns drawing pictures. Listen to Student A's instructions and draw the pictures.

Useful language

Start with a …	draw	a circle	in the middle
Then …	make	a line	next to the …
After that, …	put	a square	under the …
Finally, …	add	a triangle	at the top

1.

2.

3.

4.

5.

6.

7.

Now give instructions to Student A so that he or she can draw the pictures below.

1.

2.

3.

4.

5.

6.

7.

Show your pictures to Student A. Look at Student A's pictures. How did he or she do? Share your pictures with the rest of the class.

PRONUNCIATION

A. Numbers ending in *-teen* and *-ty*, for example, 14 and 40, can sound very similar.

Listen to these numbers:

14	40
15	50
16	60

One difference is the stress. Listen to the stress in these numbers:

thir**teen**	**thir**ty
fif**teen**	**fif**ty
eigh**teen**	**eigh**ty

The other difference is that the *t* in *-ty* words sounds like a *d*. Listen for the *d* sound:

four**teen**	**for**dy
six**teen**	**six**dy
eigh**teen**	**eigh**dy

B. Listen and circle the correct number.

1. 50   15

2. 14   40

3. 30   13

4. 1829   8029

5. 40.19   40.90

C. Practice these conversations with a classmate. Circle the number you hear.

1. **A:** How many copies do you want?

   B: Please make (16) (60) copies.

2. **A:** How long should I set the VCR for?

   B: Set it for (50) (15) minutes.

3. **A:** How many people should I invite to the party?

   B: Order invitations for (13) (30) guests.

CHALLENGE

A. You will learn how to do a card trick. You need a deck of 52 cards. First, watch your teacher follow the instructions and do the card trick. Then follow the instructions you hear.

This vocabulary will be useful. Your teacher will explain it to you.

shuffle	J = Jack = 11
deck	Q = Queen = 12
pile	K = King = 13
turn over	A = Ace = 1
count	face up/face down

STEP ONE

STEP TWO

STEP THREE

STEP FOUR

STEP FIVE

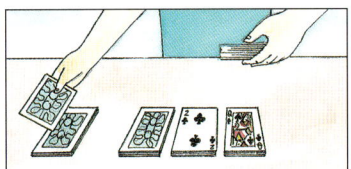

STEP SIX

What number did you get? Did the trick work?

B. Do you know a card trick that you can teach the class?

C. Read the instructions below. Can you guess what the activity is?
First, enter the booth and close the curtain.
Next, make sure the seat is the right height.
Sit down and put in your money.
Smile.
Wait for the flash (three times)!
Finally, step out of the booth and wait three minutes.

Work with a classmate. Write down instructions for another activity.

_____
_____
_____
_____
_____
_____

Read out your instructions to the class. Can they guess the activity?

Listen and repeat.

Excuse me. How do I get to the library?

Go down that sidewalk and then you'll come to the library.

Do you know where registration is?

Do you know where I pay my tuition?

It's to the right of that tall building over there.

Yes, you have to go to the registrar's office.

CONVERSATION

Listen and practice.

Minako:	Excuse me. Do you know where registration is?
Bill:	Sure. You see that tall building over there?
Minako:	Uh-huh.
Bill:	It's the shorter building to the right of it.
Minako:	Oh, thank you. Do you also know where I pay my tuition?
Bill:	Yes, you have to go to the registrar's office.
Minako:	Where's that?
Bill:	It's behind us. You have to go down that sidewalk.
Minako:	Uh-huh.
Bill:	And then you'll come to the library.
Minako:	OK.
Bill:	And then you turn right and go to the red brick building next door. The registrar's office is on the 3rd floor.
Minako:	Great. Thanks for all your help.
Bill:	Say, I could show you around campus later.
Minako:	Thanks, but I'm having dinner with my boyfriend.
Bill:	OK. Well, good luck. See you later.

PRACTICE

Work with a classmate. Look at the map and practice the dialogue.

A: Do you know where the

_____ is?

B: It's _____ .

to your right
to your left
straight ahead

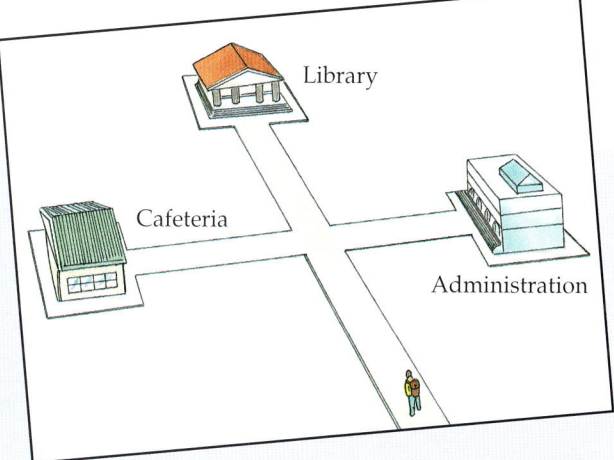

LISTEN

Listen. Match the numbers of the conversations to the pictures.

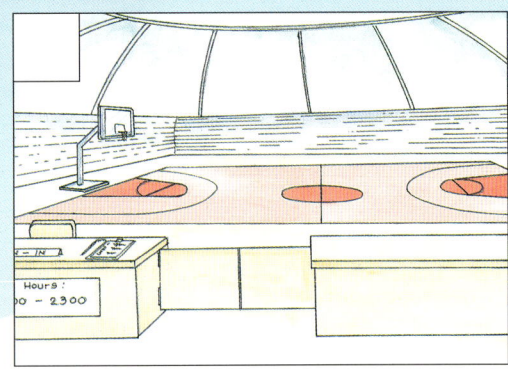

LISTEN AND UNDERSTAND

Listen to the conversation. Check the places the man has already found.

☐ registrar's office
☐ lost and found
☐ testing center
☐ student activities center
☐ video store
☐ computer lab
☐ financial aid office

☐ bookstore
☐ library
☐ gym
☐ cafeteria
☐ student lounge
☐ language lab
☐ sports field

You are going to take a few English classes at World International College. Look at the map. You and Student B have different information. Ask Student B for the missing information and complete your map. Ask about these places:

Room 114
the Student Lounge
the Registration Office
the Financial Aid Office
the Language Lab
the Computer Lab

Useful language:

Where is ...?/How do I get to ...?

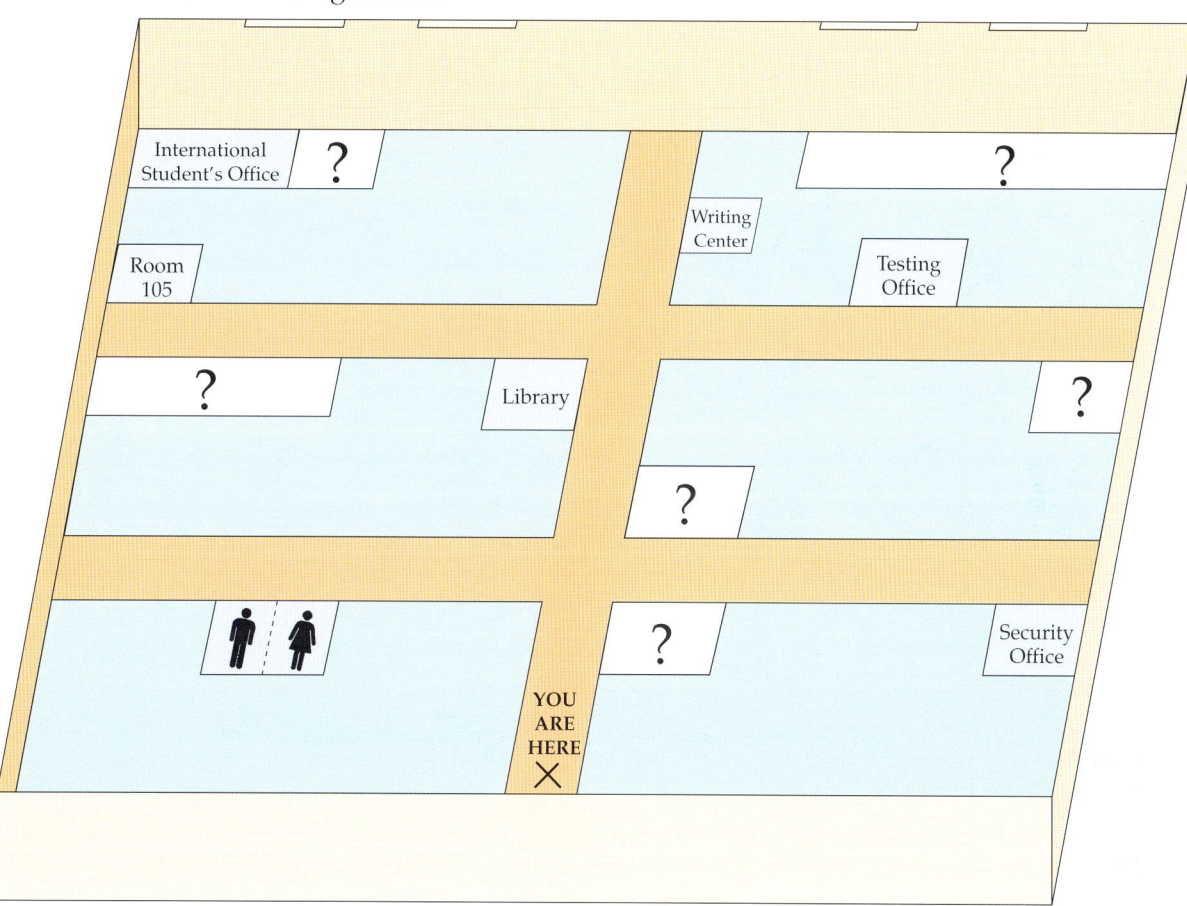

Now Student B is going to ask you about places on your map. Answer his or her questions.

Useful language:

It's straight ahead/down the hall.
It's next to/near the ...
It's to your right/left.
Turn right/left.

PAIRWORK
STUDENT B

You are going to take a few English classes at World International College. Look at the map. You and Student A have different information. Student A is going to ask you about places on your map. Answer his or her questions.

Useful language:

It's straight ahead/down the hall.
It's next to/near the ...
It's to your right/left.
Turn right/left.

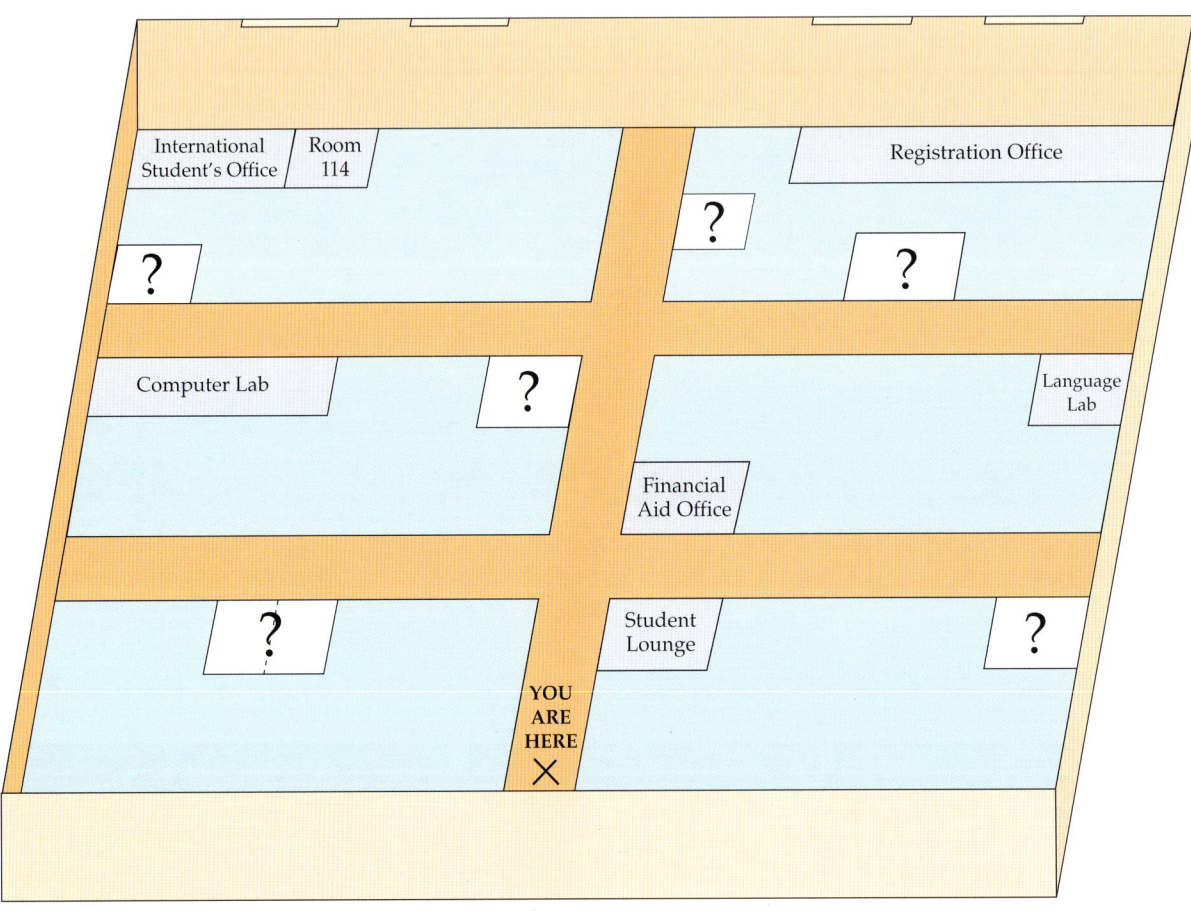

Now ask Student A for the missing information and complete your map. Ask about these places:

Room 105
the Library
the Security Office
the Testing Office
the Writing Center
the Restrooms

Useful language:

Where is ...?/How do I get to ...?

PRONUNCIATION

A. As you learned before, the intonation of *wh-* questions goes down at the end. Listen to the examples.

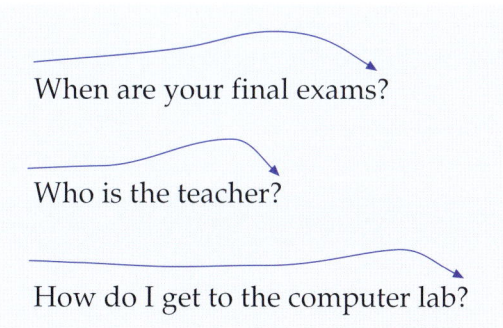

When are your final exams?

Who is the teacher?

How do I get to the computer lab?

B. Listen to these questions. Put a check next to the ones that have the intonation pattern below.

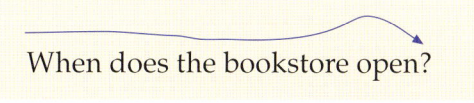

When does the bookstore open?

1. ☐ Can I sign up for Tennis 101?
2. ☐ When is the last day of the quarter?
3. ☐ Do you give early final exams?
4. ☐ How do I get to the student lounge?
5. ☐ Can I smoke in the cafeteria?
6. ☐ Is this the financial aid office?
7. ☐ What time does the lost and found close?
8. ☐ Where can I get a schedule of classes?

C. Practice pronouncing these questions with a classmate.

1. What is my grade so far?
2. When does the semester end?
3. Where's the restroom?
4. How do I get to the student lounge?
5. Where can I register?
6. Where is Room 216?
7. What days does the class meet?
8. What is the tuition?

CHALLENGE

A. What kinds of stores do you like? What kind of store do you wish your city had? You are going to design a mall you'd like to shop in. Work with a classmate. Think of ten stores. Draw them in the box below. Design the mall. Use your imagination!

B. Work with another pair. First, describe your mall. Your partners will draw it. Draw their mall below.

C. Take turns. Tell your partners how to get to some place in the mall. Your partner will guess the place.

Example: Start at the chocolate ice cream store. Go straight. It's two stores past the CD store.

Listen and repeat.

I'm bored.	Why are you bored?
I don't know. Maybe it's the time of the year.	Maybe we should have a party.
Good idea. Everyone could bring something.	I could buy some pizza.

CONVERSATION

Listen and practice.

Nicole: I'm really bored.

Dave: Me, too. Let's go to the mall. I want to look for a good book to read this weekend.

Nicole: Good idea. My brother's birthday is next week. I should get him a present. Maybe I'll get him a CD. He's been listening to a lot of classical music lately.

Dave: I don't mind classical. I listen to it sometimes, too. So why are you bored?

Nicole: I don't know. Maybe it's the time of year. When we get new classes, maybe I'll be excited again.

Dave: Yeah, you need something to look forward to. Maybe we should have a party.

Nicole: That's a good idea! We could throw a party for my brother's birthday! Everyone could bring something.

Dave: Yeah. Maybe I'll bake a cake.

Nicole: You're joking!

Dave: Yeah, I am.

PRACTICE

Work with a classmate. Look at the conversation. How many changes can you make in five minutes? Write them below:

Old	New
I'm bored.	*I'm happy.*

LISTEN

Listen to the conversations and read the sentences. Circle the correct answers.

Conversation 1

1. She wants to get a job in a restaurant.   yes   no

2. She's good with people.   yes   no

3. She's not very good at math.   yes   no

4. She likes fashion.   yes   no

Conversation 2

1. She feels happy.   yes   no

2. He is trying to cheer her up.   yes   no

3. Both people are doing well at their jobs.   yes   no

4. They're going to go to a movie.   yes   no

Conversation 3

1. He orders vegetables.   yes   no

2. He orders chicken rice.   yes   no

3. He orders steamed rice.   yes   no

4. He orders a drink.   yes   no

GROUP WORK

A. **Work in groups of three. Think of a famous person for each of the words. Join another group. Did you choose the same people?**

tense	happy	excited	energetic
depressed	tired	sad	relaxed

B. **Work in groups of three. Teach your group how to do something. Here are some examples:**

folding paper into animal shapes
doing a magic trick
playing a game
getting a date
figuring out a math problem
communicating in sign language
using a machine
cooking a special meal

C. **Work in groups of three. Choose one of your classmates for each of these jobs.**

Job	Why we chose him or her
clothing sales clerk	_____
disk jockey	_____
teacher	_____
race car driver	_____
actor	_____
tour guide	_____
waiter/waitress	_____

Around Town II

 **W**ork in groups of four. Each person places a chip on START. Take turns to throw the die and move your chip. Answer the question or follow the instruction.

1 **START** →	**2** You're at a fast food restaurant. Order lunch. Choose someone to be a waiter/waitress.	**3** Think of the last time you went shopping. What did you buy?
12 What's in your refrigerator at home?	**11** What's your favorite fast food meal?	**10** What kinds of clothing brands do you like? Name three kinds.
13 You just won $100. What are you going to buy? →	**14** When were you last sick? What was the problem?	**15** What's your favorite kind of music?
24 Tell someone how to make your favorite meal.	**23** What kind of music don't you care for?	**22** Compare yourself to someone else in the group.
25 What kind of job would you not be good at? Why? →	**26** What kind of job would you be good at? Why?	**27** What do you do when you are sad?

4 Tell someone how to get to your home.	**5** What are two things you will remember about this class?	**6** What skills do you need to be a DJ?
9 What are three jobs that are good for outgoing people?	**8** Describe the personality of your favorite actor or singer.	**7** Explain how to do something you can do well.
16 Say three words that describe your personality.	**17** What are three jobs that are good for shy people?	**18** What are the names of five medical problems in English?
21 Explain how to do something you learned recently.	**20** What kind of job would you like?	**19** Describe how to get from the school to some place else. Don't say the name. The group guesses.
28 What are you most interested in?	**29** When were you last embarrassed? Why?	**30** Play again. Go backwards this time.

Group Work

The class is almost finished. Take some time to say good-bye to your classmates. Where will they be next month? Write down their addresses. Write down their plans for next month. What do you want to remember about them?

Class Directory

Name	Address	Classmate's plans for next month	Something you will remember about your classmate

christmas Festival - Lincoln Square
10 - 5   5 $

christmas parade - Saturday downtown champagin
near West Side Park)   5:30 pm

to quit a job.
To hire / to be hired.
grief = bad

to be stopped up (like a sink)

to lay (someone off) (from a job).
to be laid off (from a job).
won't start

light won't turn on.

to fire (someone) (from job)
to be fired (lose job)